David Copperfield

Charles Dickens

retold by
Clare West

OXFORD UNIVERSITY PRESS
1994

Oxford University Press,
Walton Street, Oxford OX2 6DP

Oxford New York Toronto Madrid
Delhi Bombay Calcutta Madras Karachi
Kuala Lumpur Singapore Hong Kong Tokyo
Nairobi Dar es Salaam Cape Town
Melbourne Auckland
and associated companies in
Berlin Ibadan

OXFORD and OXFORD ENGLISH
are trade marks of Oxford University Press

ISBN 0 19 422709 X

© Oxford University Press 1994

Illustrated by Martin Hargreaves

Typeset by Wyvern Typesetting Ltd, Bristol
Printed in England by
Clays Ltd, St Ives plc

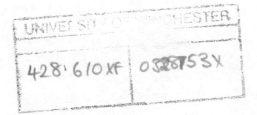

DAVID COPPERFIELD

Stage 5

'Of all my books,' wrote Charles Dickens, 'I like this the best. Like many fond parents, I have in my heart of hearts a favourite child. And his name is David Copperfield.'

Dickens himself had a difficult, unhappy childhood, and young David's life is not at all easy. His father died before he was born, and when he is eight, his mother marries again. Her new husband, Mr Murdstone, is stern and cruel, and so is his disagreeable sister, the stony-faced Miss Murdstone. As he grows up, David meets many unpleasant people – cruel schoolmasters, wicked friends, and the evil Uriah Heep, with his oily smile.

But there are other people in David's life too. There is Peggotty, his kind loving nurse, and slow Mr Barkis, a man of very few words. There is David's aunt, who tries hard to be stern but who has a heart of gold. There are the unlucky Micawbers, cheerful and despairing by turns, always waiting for something to 'turn up'. There is quiet gentle Agnes, always a true and wise friend. And then there is Dora, the loveliest girl you ever saw, with her golden hair and blue eyes – sweet, pretty, silly Dora . . .

Charles Dickens (1812–70) is one of England's greatest novelists. Born into a poor family (his father was once imprisoned for debt), Dickens became both rich and famous during his lifetime.

OXFORD BOOKWORMS

OXFORD BOOKWORMS

For a full list of titles in all the Oxford Bookworms series,
please refer to the *Oxford English* catalogue.

～ Black Series ～

Titles available include:

～**Stage 1** (400 headwords)
*The Elephant Man *Tim Vicary*
*The Monkey's Paw *W. W. Jacobs*
Under the Moon *Rowena Akinyemi*
The Phantom of the Opera *Jennifer Bassett*

～**Stage 2** (700 headwords)
*Sherlock Holmes Short Stories
  Sir Arthur Conan Doyle
*Voodoo Island *Michael Duckworth*
New Yorkers *O.Henry* (short stories)

～**Stage 3** (1000 headwords)
*Skyjack! *Tim Vicary*
Love Story *Erich Segal*
Tooth and Claw *Saki* (short stories)
Wyatt's Hurricane *Desmond Bagley*

～**Stage 4** (1400 headwords)
*The Hound of the Baskervilles
  Sir Arthur Conan Doyle
*Three Men in a Boat *Jerome K. Jerome*
The Big Sleep *Raymond Chandler*

～**Stage 5** (1800 headwords)
*Ghost Stories *retold by Rosemary Border*
The Dead of Jericho *Colin Dexter*
Wuthering Heights *Emily Brontë*
I, Robot *Isaac Asimov* (short stories)

～**Stage 6** (2500 headwords)
*Tess of the d'Urbervilles *Thomas Hardy*
Cry Freedom *John Briley*
Meteor *John Wyndham* (short stories)
Deadheads *Reginald Hill*

Many other titles available, both classic and modern.
*Cassettes available for these titles.

～ Green Series ～

Adaptations of classic and modern stories for younger readers.
Titles available include:

～**Stage 2** (700 headwords)
Robinson Crusoe *Daniel Defoe*
Alice's Adventures in Wonderland *Lewis Carroll*
Too Old to Rock and Roll *Jan Mark* (short stories)

～**Stage 3** (1000 headwords)
The Prisoner of Zenda *Anthony Hope*
The Secret Garden *Frances Hodgson Burnett*
On the Edge *Gillian Cross*

～**Stage 4** (1400 headwords)
Treasure Island *Robert Louis Stevenson*
Gulliver's Travels *Jonathan Swift*
A Tale of Two Cities *Charles Dickens*
The Silver Sword *Ian Serraillier*

OXFORD BOOKWORMS COLLECTION

Fiction by well-known authors, both classic and modern.
Texts are not abridged or simplified in any way. Titles available include:

From the Cradle to the Grave
  (short stories by *Saki, Evelyn Waugh, Roald Dahl,*
  Susan Hill, Somerset Maugham, H. E. Bates,
  Frank Sargeson, Raymond Carver)

Crime Never Pays
  (short stories by *Agatha Christie,*
  Graham Greene, Ruth Rendell, Angela Noel,
  Dorothy L. Sayers, Margery Allingham,
  Sir Arthur Conan Doyle, Patricia Highsmith)

1

David Copperfield's childhood

I was born at Blunderstone, in Suffolk, in the east of England, and was given my poor father's name, David Copperfield. Sadly, he never saw me. He was much older than my mother when they married, and died six months before I was born. My father's death made my beautiful young mother very unhappy, and she knew she would find life extremely difficult with a new baby and no husband.

The richest and most important person in our family was my father's aunt, Miss Betsey Trotwood. She had in fact been married once, to a handsome young husband. But because he demanded money from her, and sometimes beat her, she decided they should separate. He went abroad, and soon news came of his death. Miss Trotwood bought a small house by the sea, and lived there alone, with only one servant.

She had not spoken to my father since his marriage, because she considered he had made a mistake in marrying a very young girl. But just before I was born, when she heard that my mother was expecting a baby, she came to visit Blunderstone.

It was a cold, windy Friday afternoon in March. My mother was sitting by the fire, feeling very lonely and unhappy, and crying a little. Suddenly a stern, strange-looking face appeared at the window.

'Open the door!' ordered the stern-faced lady.

My mother was shocked, but obeyed at once.

'You must be David Copperfield's wife,' said the lady as she entered. 'I'm Betsey Trotwood. You've heard of me?'

'Yes,' whispered my mother, trembling.

'How young you are!' cried Miss Betsey. 'Just a baby!'

My mother started sobbing again. 'I know I look like a child! I know I was young to be a wife, and I'm young to be a mother! But perhaps I'll die before I become a mother!'

'Come, come!' answered Miss Betsey. 'Have some tea. Then you'll feel better. What do you call your girl?'

'My girl? I don't know yet that it will be a girl,' replied my mother miserably.

'No, I don't mean the baby, I mean your servant!'

'Her name's Peggotty. Her first name's Clara, the same as mine, so I call her by her family name, you see.'

'What a terrible name! However, never mind. Peggotty!' she called, going to the door. 'Bring Mrs Copperfield some tea at once!' She sat down again and continued speaking. 'You were talking about the baby. I'm sure it'll be a girl. Now, as soon as she's born . . .'

'He, perhaps,' said my mother bravely.

'Don't be stupid, of course it'll be a *she*. I'm going to send her to school, and educate her well. I want to prevent her from making the mistakes *I've* made in life.' Miss Betsey looked quite angry as she said this. My mother said nothing, as she was not feeling at all well. 'But tell me, were you and your husband happy?' asked Miss Betsey.

This made my poor mother feel worse than ever. 'I know I wasn't very sensible – about money – or cooking – or things like that!' she sobbed. 'But we loved each other – and he was helping me to learn – and then he died! Oh! Oh!' And she fell back in her chair, completely unconscious.

Peggotty, who came in just then with the tea, realized how

serious the situation was, and took my mother upstairs to bed. The doctor arrived soon afterwards, and stayed all evening to take care of his patient.

At about midnight he came downstairs to the sitting-room where Miss Betsey was waiting impatiently.

'Well, doctor, what's the news? How is she?'

'The young mother is quite comfortable, madam,' replied the doctor politely.

'But *she*, the baby, how is *she*?' cried Miss Betsey.

The doctor looked strangely at Miss Betsey. 'It's a boy, madam,' he replied.

Miss Betsey said nothing, but walked straight out of the house, and never came back.

That was how I was born. My early childhood was extremely happy, as my beautiful mother and kind Peggotty took care of me. But when I was about eight, a shadow passed over my happiness. My mother often went out walking, in her best clothes, with a gentleman called Mr Murdstone. He had black hair, a big black moustache and an unpleasant smile, and seemed to be very fond of my mother. But I knew that Peggotty did not like him.

A few months later Peggotty told me that my mother was going to have a short holiday with some friends. Meanwhile Peggotty and I would go to stay with her brother Daniel in Yarmouth, on the east coast, for two weeks. I was very excited when we climbed into the cart, although it was sad saying goodbye to my mother. Mr Murdstone was at her shoulder, waving goodbye, as the driver called to his horse, and we drove out of the village.

When we got down from the cart in Yarmouth, after our journey, Peggotty said, 'That's the house, Master David!'

I looked all round, but could only see an old ship on the sand. 'Is that – that your brother's house?' I asked in delight. And when we reached it, I saw it had doors and windows and a chimney, just like a real house. I could not imagine a nicer place to live. Everything was clean and tidy, and smelt of fish. Now I was introduced to the Peggotty family. There was Daniel Peggotty, a kind old sailor. Although he was not married, he had adopted two orphans, who lived with him and called him Uncle. Ham Peggotty was a large young man with a gentle smile, and Emily was a beautiful, blue-eyed little girl. They all welcomed Peggotty and me warmly.

I spent a wonderfully happy two weeks there, playing all day on the beach with Emily, and sleeping in my own little bed on the ship. I am sure I was in love with little Emily in my childish way, and I cried bitterly when we had to say goodbye at the end of the holiday.

But on the way home to Blunderstone, Peggotty looked at me very worriedly. 'Master David, my dear,' she said suddenly in a trembling voice. 'I must tell you – you'll have to know now . . . While we've been away, your dear mother – has married Mr Murdstone! He's your stepfather now!'

I was deeply shocked. I could not understand how my mother could have married that man. And when we arrived home, I could not help showing my mother how very miserable I was. I went straight to my room and lay sobbing on my bed, which made my poor mother very unhappy too. As she sat beside me, holding my hand, Mr Murdstone suddenly came in.

'What's this, Clara, my love?' he asked sternly. 'Remember, you must be firm with the boy! I've told you before, you're too weak with him!'

'Oh yes, Edward, I'm afraid you're right,' my mother replied quickly. 'I'm very sorry. I'll try to be firmer with him.'

And when she left the room, Mr Murdstone whispered angrily to me, 'David, do you know what I'll do if you don't obey me? I'll beat you like a dog!'

I was still very young, and I was very frightened of him. If he had said one kind word to me, perhaps I would have liked and trusted him, and my life would have been different. Instead, I hated him for the influence he had over my dear mother, who wanted to be kind to me, but also wanted to please her new husband.

That evening Mr Murdstone's sister arrived to 'help' my mother in the house. A tall dark lady, with a stern, frowning face, she looked and sounded very much like her brother. I thought she was planning to stay with us for a long time, and I was right. In fact, she intended to stay for ever. She started work the next morning.

'Now, Clara,' she said firmly to my mother at breakfast, 'I am here to help you. You're much too pretty and thoughtless to worry about the servants, the food and so on. So just hand me your keys to all the cupboards, and I'll take care of everything for you.'

My poor mother just blushed, looked a little ashamed, and obeyed. From then on, Miss Murdstone took complete control of the house, keeping the keys hanging from her waist as she hurried through the house, checking that everything was being done just as she wished.

2

David is sent away to school

I was very unhappy during this time. Mr Murdstone insisted on my studying, and so my mother gave me lessons. In the past she and I had enjoyed our studies together, and she had taught me a lot in her gentle way. But now both Mr and Miss Murdstone were present during my lessons, and somehow I could not concentrate or remember what I had learnt. My poor mother was very sympathetic, and tried to encourage me, sometimes even whispering the answer to me. But the Murdstones had sharp ears.

'Clara, my love!' Mr Murdstone used to say crossly. 'Remember! Be firm! You're making the boy's character worse by helping him like that!'

'Oh Edward, I'm sorry,' my mother replied, looking embarrassed and hanging her head like a guilty child.

One morning when I arrived in the sitting-room as usual for my lesson, I saw that Mr Murdstone had a thin stick in his hand. I could not take my eyes off it.

'You must be *very* careful today, David,' he said with his unpleasant smile, holding the stick in both hands.

I knew what would happen then. A terrible fear took hold of me, and all that I had learnt disappeared immediately from my memory, so that I could not answer any of my mother's questions. Mr Murdstone got up from his chair.

'Well, David,' he said heavily, 'I think you've worried your mother enough today. We'll go upstairs, boy. Come,' and he picked up the stick. I heard my mother crying as we went upstairs.

'Please, Mr Murdstone!' I cried. 'Don't beat me! I've tried to

'*You must be* very *careful today, David.*'

learn, really I have, sir!'

But he did not listen to me. In my bedroom, he held my arms and started hitting me with the stick. I managed to get hold of his hand, and bit deep into it. He cried out angrily, and began to hit me as hard as he could. Above the noise of my screams, I could hear my mother and Peggotty crying outside the door. Then the next moment, he was gone. I heard him lock the door. And I was lying, sore and bleeding, on the floor. The whole house seemed suddenly very quiet.

I stayed there for a time, without moving. In the evening Miss Murdstone brought me some bread and milk, which she left on the floor beside me, frowning angrily at me as she went out. I was kept locked in that room for five days and nights, and saw nobody except Miss Murdstone, who brought me food but never spoke to me. To a small boy, the five days seemed like years, and I can still remember how frightened and guilty I felt.

But during the fifth night I heard a strange noise at the keyhole. It was Peggotty, trying to give me a message.

'Master David, my dear,' she whispered, sobbing, 'they're going to send you away to boarding school! Tomorrow!'

'Oh Peggotty!' I cried. 'Then I won't see you and mother very often!'

'No, my love. But don't forget, I'll take care of your mother. She needs her cross old Peggotty! I'll stay with her, although I hate these Murdstones. And remember, David, I love you as much as I love your mother, and more. And I'll write to you.'

'Thank you, dear Peggotty!' I whispered back, tears rolling down my face. 'Will you write to your brother too, and Ham, and little Emily, and tell them I'm not as bad as the Murdstones think? And send my love to them, especially little Emily?'

Peggotty promised to do what I asked. The next morning Miss Murdstone told me that because of my wickedness I was going away to school. She had already packed my case for me. My mother was only allowed to say a very quick goodbye to me, when the horse and cart arrived. The driver put my case on the cart, and we drove slowly out of Blunderstone.

I was still sobbing loudly when suddenly I saw Peggotty running after us on the road. The driver stopped and waited for her. With difficulty she climbed up onto the cart.

'Here, Master David!' she cried breathlessly. 'A little present from me and your dear mother! Take care of yourself, my dear!' She put a small purse and a paper bag into my hands, and held me so close to her fat body that I thought I would never breathe again. Then she jumped down and ran back along the road to the village.

As we continued our journey, I dried my tears and looked at what she had given me. The bag was full of Peggotty's special cakes, and in the purse were eight bright shilling coins. Thinking of my mother and Peggotty made me start crying again, but just then the driver, Mr Barkis, began to talk to me. He was a large, red-faced man, who clearly found conversation difficult.

'Did *she* make those cakes?' he asked slowly, having finished the one that I had offered him.

'You mean Peggotty, sir? Yes, she does all our cooking.'

'*Does* she?' replied Mr Barkis with great interest. There was a long silence while he considered his next question.

'Does she have a young man?' he asked. 'You know, someone who wants to marry her?'

'Peggotty? A young man?' I repeated, surprised. 'Oh no, she's never had any young men.'

'Ah!' replied Mr Barkis, looking very pleased. Again he thought for a long time before speaking.

'Well,' he said at last, 'perhaps if you write to her – will you be writing to her? You could give her a message from me. You could say "Barkis is willing". Would you do that?'

'"Barkis is willing",' I repeated innocently, wondering what the message meant. 'Yes, of course. But you could tell her yourself, Mr Barkis, when you return to Blunderstone tomorrow.'

'No, no,' he said, 'no, you just give her the message. Remember, "Barkis is willing".'

After this conversation Mr Barkis was completely silent for the rest of the journey. When we arrived in Yarmouth, I bought paper at the hotel and wrote this letter to Peggotty:

My dear Peggotty,
I have arrived safely in Yarmouth. Barkis is willing.
Please give my love to mother.
Yours, David
P.S. He says it's important – *Barkis is willing*.

In Yarmouth I was put on the long-distance coach to London, and travelled all through the night. At the coach station in London I was collected by a teacher, Mr Mell, and taken to Salem House, the school which the Murdstones had chosen for me.

The school was a large old building with a dusty playground, surrounded by a high brick wall. It looked strangely deserted. I was very surprised to find that none of the boys were there, and was told that they were all on holiday, and that I had been sent there during the holidays as a punishment for my wickedness. The headmaster and teachers were on holiday too, all except for Mr Mell, who had to look after me.

I spent a whole month in that miserable place, doing my lessons in the dirty, empty classroom, which smelt of old food and unwashed boys. Every evening I had to eat my supper with Mr Mell, and then go straight to bed. The worst thing was the sign I had to wear round my neck. It said: BE CAREFUL! HE BITES. I was only allowed to take it off when I went to bed.

Although I was extremely lonely and unhappy at this time, I was not looking forward to meeting all the other boys. I felt sure they would laugh at me and especially at the sign I was forced to wear. But one day Mr Mell told me that the headmaster, Mr Creakle, had returned, and wanted to see me. So I went, trembling, to his part of the house.

I realized at once that Mr Creakle lived much more comfortably than the boys or the teachers. He was a small, fat man with a purple nose, who was sitting in an armchair with a bottle and a glass in front of him.

'So, this is the boy who bites, is it?' he asked unpleasantly. 'I know your stepfather, boy. He's a man of strong character, he is. He knows me, and I know him. Do *you* know me? Answer me, boy!' He pulled violently at my ear.

'Not yet, sir,' I answered, tears of pain in my eyes.

'Ah, but you soon will! Oh yes, I have a strong character too, you'll see!' He banged his hand hard on the table.

I was very frightened, but I made myself ask the question I had been considering for a whole month. 'Please, sir, I'm very sorry for what I did to Mr Murdstone. Could – could I take this sign off, before the other boys see it . . .'

Mr Creakle gave a sudden, terrible shout and jumped out of his chair. I did not wait to see whether he was going to hit me, but ran out of his room and hid in my bed for the next hour.

11

However, the boys were not as cruel to me as I had feared. I made a friend almost immediately, a boy called Tommy Traddles, who was known to be the unluckiest boy in the school. I was also noticed, and even smiled on, by the great James Steerforth, one of the oldest boys, at least six years older than me. He was a handsome, intelligent, curly-haired young man, who had become an important figure at the school, with great influence over the younger boys.

'How much money have you got, Copperfield?' he asked me.

'Eight shillings, Steerforth,' I answered, remembering the present my mother and Peggotty had given me.

'You'd better give it to me. I'll take care of it for you,' he offered in a friendly way.

I opened Peggotty's purse and turned it upside-down into his hand.

'Perhaps you'd like to spend some of it now?' he suggested, smiling. 'A bottle of wine, a tin of biscuits, a few cakes, that sort of thing? I can go out whenever I like, so I can buy it for you.'

'Ye-es, that's very kind of you,' I said, although I was a little worried that all my money would disappear.

When we went upstairs to bed, I realized that all my money *had* been spent, as eight shillings' worth of food and drink was laid out on my bed in the moonlight. Of course I did not want to eat and drink it all by myself, so I invited Steerforth and the others to help themselves. The boys were very willing, and we spent a pleasant evening, sitting on our beds, whispering to each other. I discovered that the boys all hated Salem House, which they considered one of the worst schools in the country. They especially hated Mr Creakle, who was in the habit of beating them regularly with a heavy stick which he carried with him at all times.

The only boy he dared not beat was Steerforth. I admired Steerforth even more when I heard this.

When we were all too tired to stay awake, Steerforth got up to go. 'Goodnight, young Copperfield,' he said, putting a hand on my head. 'I'll take care of you.'

'It's very kind of you,' I replied gratefully.

'You haven't got a sister, have you?' he asked sleepily.

'No, I haven't,' I answered.

'What a pity! If you had one, I'm sure she'd be a pretty, bright-eyed little girl. I would have liked to meet her.'

I thought of him a lot that night, with his laughing, handsome face, and his careless, confident manner. I could never have imagined what a dark shadow he would throw over the lives of people who were dear to me.

I stayed at Salem House for three more months. Although one or two of the teachers, like Mr Mell, were kind to us boys, and tried to teach us properly, we were too afraid of Mr Creakle and his stick to concentrate on our studies. But Tommy Traddles and I cheered each other up if we were beaten, and I was lucky enough to be friendly with the great Steerforth, in spite of the difference in our ages.

However, my home, even with the Murdstones there, seemed a much pleasanter place than school, and I was glad when the Christmas holidays arrived, and I was allowed to return to Blunderstone. I was a little surprised to find that my mother had a new baby, and I could see at once that she was not well. She looked tired and worried, and very thin. But she and Peggotty were delighted to see me, although they dared not show it if the Murdstones were present. My stepfather and his sister seemed to hate me even more than before, if that were possible, and they

13

made my life quite miserable whenever they could. In fact, I was almost pleased when it was time to return to school, and see Traddles and Steerforth again.

As the cart drove away, I remember my mother standing outside our house, with her baby in her arms, smiling sadly at me. That was the last time I saw her, and that is how I shall always remember her.

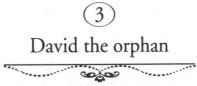

David the orphan

Life went on as normal for me at school, until my birthday two months later in March. I remember that day very well. It was cold, icy weather, and we boys had to blow on our fingers and rub our hands to keep warm in the freezing classrooms. When a message came for me to go and see Mr Creakle, I thought that Peggotty must have sent me a birthday present, and so I hurried gladly along to his room. But there I realized something unusual had happened, because it was Mr Creakle's wife who was waiting to speak to me.

'David, my child,' she said kindly, holding my hand, 'we all have to accept that our loved ones can die at any moment.'

I looked at her, trying to understand what she meant.

'I'm sorry to tell you,' she continued, 'that your mother is dangerously ill.'

There was a mist in front of my eyes, and suddenly burning tears ran down my face. I knew the truth.

'Your mother is dead,' she said.

I was already sobbing loudly and I felt I was an orphan, quite

*That was the last time I saw her, and that
is how I shall always remember her.*

alone in the world.

Mrs Creakle packed my case herself, and sent me home on the coach for the funeral. I did not realize at the time that I would never return to Salem House.

When I arrived home, Peggotty met me at the door, and we cried miserably in each other's arms. Mr Murdstone seemed very sad, and did not speak to me at all. Miss Murdstone, however, showed her usual firmness of character (which she and her brother were so proud of) by checking that I had brought all my clothes back from school. After that she showed no interest in me at all. There was a deathly stillness in the house. Peggotty took me up to the room where my dear mother's dead body lay, with my little brother, who had died a few hours after her. Everything was fresh and clean in the room, but I could not look at my mother's lovely face, which would never smile at me again, without crying.

'How did it happen, Peggotty?' I asked, sobbing.

'She was ill for a long time, Master David. She got worse after the baby was born, you see. She was sometimes unhappy and forgetful, but she was always the same to me, her old Peggotty. Those two downstairs often spoke crossly to her and made her sad, but she still loved them, you know – she was so sweet and loving! I always sat beside her while she went to sleep. It made her feel better, she said.' There was a short silence while Peggotty dried her eyes, then took both my hands in hers. 'On the last night, she asked me for some water, and then gave me such a patient smile! She looked so beautiful! The sun was beginning to rise, and she put her head on my arm, on her stupid cross old Peggotty's arm, and died like an innocent child going to sleep!'

After my mother's funeral, I began to wonder what would happen to me. The Murdstones did not even seem to notice that I was in the house. They had told Peggotty to leave, as they did not want her as their servant any more, so Peggotty was going to her brother's in Yarmouth, until she decided what work to do next. She suggested taking me with her for a holiday, and to my surprise the Murdstones agreed.

So next morning Mr Barkis appeared at the door with his cart, and Peggotty's cases were put on it. We climbed up and sat beside him. Peggotty was naturally a little sad to leave her old home, where she had been so happy with my mother and me, and at first she cried a little. But when Mr Barkis saw her drying her eyes and looking more cheerful, he too began to look happier, and he whispered to me, 'Barkis is willing! *You* told her that!' Aloud he said to Peggotty, 'Are you comfortable?'

Peggotty laughed and said that she was.

'And are *you* comfortable, Master David?' he asked.

I said that I was. Mr Barkis was so pleased with this conversation that he repeated it many times during the journey, and Peggotty and I both had to keep giving him the same answer.

When we arrived in Yarmouth and got down from the cart, we said goodbye to Mr Barkis. Daniel and Ham Peggotty were waiting for us. Daniel and Ham were exactly the same as I remembered them, cheerful and generous as ever, but little Emily seemed different somehow. She was taller and prettier, but she did not want to play with me, or spend her time with me. I was rather disappointed, because I still considered she was the most beautiful girl I had ever seen, and I thought I was in love with her. Daniel and Ham were very proud of her intelligence and beauty, and just smiled when she laughingly refused to sit next to me. But they all listened with interest to my stories of school life at Salem House. I told them about the other boys, especially the handsome, clever Steerforth. I admired him so much that I could not stop myself telling them all about him. Suddenly I noticed that Emily was listening eagerly, her blue eyes shining and a smile on her lips. She blushed when she saw that we were all looking at her, and hid her face behind her hands.

'Emily's like me,' said Peggotty kindly, 'and would like to see David's friend Mr Steerforth.'

The days passed happily, although Emily and I did not play together as we had done before. Mr Barkis was a frequent visitor, and soon Peggotty explained to me that she had decided to marry him.

'I'll love you just as much, David, my dear, when I'm married!' she told me, holding me close to her. 'And I'll be able to come and see you in the cart any time I like. Barkis is a good man and I'm sure I'll be happy with him. He's got a nice little house, and I'll keep a little bedroom there for you to use whenever you want. You'll always be welcome to come and stay!'

So when I returned to Blunderstone, Peggotty had become Mrs Barkis, and I was glad to think of her in her own house, with a husband to take care of her. At home, my stepfather and his sister did not seem pleased to see me, and were clearly trying to find a way of getting rid of me. As they considered school too expensive, they finally arranged for me to start work, although I was still only ten years old, and very small for my age. I was sent to London, to work in a warehouse in the east of the city, near the river.

My job was to wash bottles, which would then be filled with wine, or to pack the filled bottles in cases. I was paid only six shillings a week. There were several other boys who worked with me, but I was the only one who had been to school. All the warehouse workers were coarse, rough people, who were used to working in dirty conditions for long hours. No words can describe the horror I felt, when I realized what my life was going to be like from now on. I was deeply ashamed at having such a job and I was also afraid that I would forget everything I had learnt from my mother and my teachers. I would never find friends like Traddles or Steerforth, or be able to get a better position in life. It was an extremely unhappy time for me.

My stepfather had asked Mr Quinion, the manager, to find me somewhere to stay in London, so at the end of my first day I was called to Mr Quinion's office and introduced to an important-looking, rather fat, middle-aged man with a head as bald as an egg. His name was Mr Micawber, and he offered me a spare room in the house he was renting with his family. I agreed to take it, and Mr Micawber and I walked home together.

The Micawbers were obviously very poor, but tried hard not to let this show. The house had several floors of rather dirty, empty rooms with very little furniture. Mrs Micawber was a thin, tired-looking woman with a baby in her arms. The baby was one of twins, and in all my experience of the family, I never saw Mrs Micawber without at least one of the twins. They also had a four-year-old son and a three-year-old daughter. Their only servant was a young orphan girl.

'I never thought,' Mrs Micawber told me sadly as she showed me my room, 'when I lived with Mother and Father, before I was married, that I would ever be as poor as this. But as Mr Micawber is for the moment in difficulties, I must of course accept the situation. I'm afraid he owes a lot of money, but his creditors will just have to wait! You can't get blood out of a stone, nor can anyone get any money at all out of Mr Micawber at present!'

I soon realized that neither Mr nor Mrs Micawber had ever been able to manage money. The little that Mr Micawber earned was not enough, either to keep his creditors happy, or to pay for the needs of his growing family. So his creditors were constantly at the door, demanding payment, and meals were rather irregular in the Micawber house. Mr and Mrs Micawber's moods varied according to the situation. One moment Mr Micawber looked extremely miserable and depressed, the next he was brushing his shoes and singing a song before going out. Mrs Micawber's character was similar to her husband's. Sometimes I came home to find her lying on the floor, with her hair undone, looking wild and desperate, but an hour later she was cheerfully eating a good supper.

I lived with these kind people for several months, and became very fond of them. I bought my own food out of my wages, because I knew the Micawbers hardly ever had enough for themselves, and I lived mostly on bread and cheese. As they were so short of money, once or twice I offered to lend them a few shillings, which they refused to accept. But at last Mr Micawber's creditors became tired of waiting for their money, and went to the police, who arrested him for debt. He was taken to the King's Prison, and asked me to visit him there. When I arrived, I was shown to his room, where he was waiting for me. He seemed quite broken-hearted, and even cried a little.

'This is a black day for me, Copperfield!' he sobbed. 'I hope my mistakes will be a warning to young people like you! Remember, if a man earns twenty pounds a year, and spends nineteen pounds and nineteen shillings, the result is happiness. But if he spends twenty pounds and one shilling, the result is misery! By the way, Copperfield, could you lend me a shilling for some beer? Mrs Micawber will pay you back as soon as you arrive home.'

*'But if he spends twenty pounds and one
shilling, the result is misery!'*

And when the beer arrived, he appeared much more cheerful. We had a pleasant evening, telling stories and jokes.

He stayed in prison for several weeks, and I visited him regularly. I was delighted to hear on one of my visits that he would soon be free, as his creditors had unwillingly accepted the fact that he had no way of paying his debts. I gave the news to Mrs Micawber when I returned home. We celebrated by sharing our supper and a glass of wine together.

'May I ask what you will do, madam, when Mr Micawber is free?' I asked politely.

'My family,' said Mrs Micawber grandly, 'believe that Mr Micawber should move to the country, to Devon, and carry on his business interests there. Mr Micawber is a very clever man, Master Copperfield.'

'I'm sure he is,' I agreed.

'Although they haven't found anything exactly right for him yet, my family think he should be ready, in Devon, in case something turns up.' She put down her empty glass.

'And will you be going with him, madam?' I asked.

'I must! I will!' Mrs Micawber's voice rose to a scream. 'He is my life! My love! My husband! The father of my children! I will never desert Mr Micawber! You can't ask me to desert him!'

I felt very uncomfortable, as I had not asked her to desert him at all, but she soon became calm again and finished her supper. I was becoming used to the Micawbers' changes of mood.

I now realized that when the Micawbers left London, as they were planning to do, I would be very lonely in the city. I still hated my work in the warehouse, and wanted to make a better life for myself. I thought about it for a long time, and decided there was only one thing I could do. I would try to find my one surviving relation, my father's aunt, Miss Betsey Trotwood, and ask her to help me. I knew she lived somewhere near Dover, in Kent. I could go there by coach, because Peggotty had once sent me ten shillings to keep, in case I ever needed it. The time had come to use that money.

(4)

David and his aunt

So, after helping the Micawbers to pack their few clothes, and waving goodbye to them at the coach station on their way to Devon, I went to the warehouse for my last day at work. I did not tell anyone I would not be coming back the following week. In the evening I packed my case, and put the ten shillings in the little purse Peggotty had once given me. I looked around for someone to help me with my case, which was rather heavy for me, and saw a tall young man with a horse and cart passing by.

'Could you please take my case to the coach station?' I asked him politely.

The young man put the case into his cart. Then, looking round quickly to make sure there were no witnesses, he pushed me roughly against the wall and took my purse out of my trembling hand. Before I could say a word, he had driven the horse and cart down the road and out of sight round the corner. I knew I would never see him, my case or my ten shillings again.

I sat down on the pavement and cried. Now I had lost everything I owned in the world, and had no money for the coach fare to

Dover. In the end I decided I would have to walk there, and I started the long journey. It took me six days to cover the hundred kilometres, as I got tired very easily, and had to rest. I sold my jacket for a shilling, so that I could buy bread and milk on the way, and at night I slept in disused farm buildings or under trees. Sometimes I was afraid of the dangerous-looking beggars and thieves I met on the road, but I knew I had to keep going. As I walked, I thought of my mother's gentle, pretty face. I felt sure she would approve of what I was doing, and that encouraged me to continue.

But when I arrived in Dover, it seemed a much larger town than I had imagined. I spent a whole morning asking people if they knew where Miss Betsey Trotwood lived. Finally I found someone who recognized the name and showed me the way to her house. I stood at her front door, in the neat little garden, for a few moments, trembling with fear, and wondering what my aunt would think of me. My face and hands were dirty, my hair was unbrushed, and my clothes were torn and dusty. Perhaps she wouldn't even want to invite me into her house!

Just then a handsome but strict-looking grey-haired woman came out of the door towards me. I knew she must be my aunt.

'Go away!' she said crossly. 'I don't allow anyone to walk on my grass!'

'Please, madam,' I said bravely, 'please, aunt . . .'

'WHAT?' cried Miss Betsey in great surprise.

'Please, aunt, I'm your nephew.'

'Good heavens!' she cried, and sat down rather suddenly on the grass.

'I'm David Copperfield, your nephew's son, of Blunderstone in Suffolk, where you came on the night I was born, and saw my dear mother. I've been very unhappy since she died. My stepfather sent me to work in London, and I hated it, and ran away, and someone stole my case and my money, and I've had to walk all the way, and I haven't slept in a bed for six nights!' Here my self-control broke, and I fell to the ground, sobbing bitterly.

My aunt jumped to her feet, picked me up and took me into her sitting-room, where she mixed some medicine in a glass and made me drink it. She also wrapped me in a large blanket and put me on her sofa. Then she rang the bell for her servant, Janet.

'Please ask Mr Dick to come here, Janet,' she said.

A tall, grey-haired, pleasant-looking gentleman entered a few minutes later, laughing rather strangely to himself.

'Now, Mr Dick,' said my aunt firmly, 'don't be a fool, because we all know you're intelligent.' Mr Dick looked very serious at once. 'No doubt you remember that I had a nephew, David Copperfield? Well, this is his son. He has run away.'

'Oh, really? David's son! Run away! Well!' said Mr Dick.

'Now the question is, Mr Dick, what shall I do with him?'

'Well —' Mr Dick looked vacantly at me, and then suddenly his eyes shone. 'If I were you, I would wash him!'

'Well done, Mr Dick! You always have the right answer!' said my aunt delightedly.

And so they washed me, and gave me clean clothes and delicious food. While I was eating, my aunt stared at me, occasionally whispering 'Good heavens!' to herself. When she could see that I felt better, she asked me question after question, and I told her the story of my life.

'Good heavens!' she said again, when I had finished. 'Why did your poor mother marry again? What a terrible mistake!'

'Perhaps she was in love,' suggested Mr Dick, smiling his rather foolish smile.

'In love!' said Miss Betsey crossly. 'Perhaps the poor silly girl *thought* she was in love! But now, Mr Dick, another question. What should we do with the boy?'

'Well –' said Mr Dick, thinking. Then an idea suddenly came to him. 'You should put him to bed!'

'Thank you again, Mr Dick, for your common sense!' said my aunt happily. 'Janet, put the boy to bed!'

And so, in a comfortable clean little bed, in a pleasant airy room at the top of Miss Betsey Trotwood's house, I floated away into the world of my dreams.

At breakfast next morning I bravely asked my aunt, 'Are you – have you – what's going to happen to me?'

'I've written to your stepfather,' she replied.

'Oh! Are you going to send me back to the Murdstones? Please don't, aunt! Please let me stay here!' I cried, trembling.

'I don't know what I'll do yet. We'll have to wait and see,' she answered firmly.

This news made me very depressed, but there was nothing I could do about it and my aunt soon began to talk about something else.

'What do you think of Mr Dick, child?'

'He looks a little – well, mad. Is he mad, aunt?'

'Well, his family called him mad, and wanted to lock him up for ever. But I met him, and thought – I still think – he's an extremely sensible, intelligent person. So I offered to take care of him, and he's lived in my house for ten years. Nobody knows what useful advice he's given me! I trust him completely!'

When I heard how generous my aunt had been to poor harmless Mr Dick, I began to understand her character better. In spite of her stern appearance and frequent crossness, she was very kind to people who needed her help. I hoped she would be kind to *me*.

Several days later, I was looking out of the sitting-room window when I saw Mr and Miss Murdstone riding into my aunt's garden. My aunt had seen them too, and hurried out, waving her umbrella angrily at them and shouting, 'Go away! Don't ride on my grass! Who do you think you are? Go away, I tell you!'

'Aunt!' I cried out. 'They're Mr and Miss Murdstone!'

'I don't care!' she shouted. 'Nobody is allowed to ride on my grass!' And she went back into her house, banging the door behind her. The Murdstones had to lead their horses out of the garden, and then return to ring the doorbell. They looked very uncomfortable and unsure of themselves. Janet showed them into the sitting-room, where my aunt, Mr Dick and I were waiting.

'Miss Trotwood—' began Mr Murdstone, stepping forward.

'Excuse me,' said my aunt sharply. 'I imagine you are the Mr Murdstone who married my nephew's widow. In my opinion, it would have been much better if you had never married the poor child.'

'I agree with you, Miss Trotwood,' said Miss Murdstone, smiling falsely. 'My brother would certainly have been happier if he hadn't married her, because I consider poor dear Clara was, in fact, just a child.'

'Fortunately,' said my aunt, 'you and I, madam, are too old and plain for anyone to say that about us.'

Miss Murdstone did not seem eager to agree to this. Her brother, however, wanted to get down to business.

'Miss Trotwood,' he said, a little crossly, 'having received your letter, I've come to explain to you, in case you haven't realized it yet, that this boy is extremely wicked and violent. Both my sister and I have tried to change his character, but sadly we have failed.'

'I must add,' said Miss Murdstone, 'that of all the boys in the world, I believe this is the worst boy.'

'I see,' said my aunt. 'Now tell me, has David inherited any money from his father or mother?'

'No, madam,' answered Mr Murdstone. 'My dear Clara naturally trusted me to take care of David, and I'm ready to do that, if he comes back with me now. But I alone shall decide what to do with him, Miss Trotwood – understand that. I am here, for the first and last time, to take him away. If you decide to keep him with you, you keep him for ever.'

'What do you say, David?' asked my aunt, turning to me.

'Please don't let me go with them, aunt!' I begged. 'They've always been unkind to me, and they made my mother very unhappy. I'll be so miserable if I have to go back with them!'

'What do you think, Mr Dick?' asked my aunt.

Mr Dick thought for a moment. 'Get a suit of clothes made for him immediately,' he said.

'What would I do without you, Mr Dick!' asked my aunt, shaking his hand enthusiastically. Then she turned to Mr Murdstone.

'You'd better go. I'll keep the boy and take my chance with him. I don't believe a word of your story. Do you think I don't know how you broke that poor girl's heart? And how you hated her son, and punished him for it? I can see by your face that I'm right.' We all stared at Mr Murdstone. It was true that his face was white and he was breathing fast. 'Goodbye, sir, and goodbye to you too, madam,' added my aunt, turning suddenly to Miss Murdstone. 'If I see you riding on my grass again, I'll knock your hat right off your head!'

The Murdstones said nothing in reply to these fierce words,

'*Get a suit of clothes made for him immediately.*'

but walked quickly out of the house.

'Thank you, thank you, aunt!' I cried. 'I'll do my best to make you proud of me!' and I kissed her many times.

'Mr Dick, you and I will adopt this boy together,' said my aunt, her stern expression softening into a smile.

And so a new life began for me. I was soon able to forget the warehouse and the Murdstones, in learning to please my aunt, and to play games with Mr Dick, who spent much of his time with me.

But one day my aunt suggested that I should go to boarding school in Canterbury. I was delighted, as I was eager to continue my studies, and Canterbury was very near my aunt's home in Dover. So the next day my aunt and I went to Canterbury, where I admired the beautiful old buildings in the ancient city centre.

'Is it a large school, aunt?' I asked politely.

'I haven't decided which school you'll go to yet,' she replied. 'First we're going to ask my old friend Mr Wickfield's advice about it. He lives and works in Canterbury, you see.'

Soon we stopped in front of a very old house, with a very clean front doorstep, and fresh white curtains at the windows. A strange-looking person, dressed in black, with short red hair and a very thin white face came out to meet us. I thought he must be a servant. He was about fifteen, but looked much older.

'Is Mr Wickfield at home, Uriah Heep?' asked my aunt.

'He is, madam,' replied Uriah, smiling unpleasantly. He showed us into the sitting-room, where I noticed two large paintings on the wall, one of a grey-haired gentleman and the other of a lady with a sweet, gentle face. Just then a gentleman entered the room, looking a little older than his picture. I soon discovered he was Mr Wickfield, my aunt's lawyer.

'Mr Wickfield,' said my aunt, 'this is my nephew. I have adopted him, and I want to send him to a good boarding school here in Canterbury. Can you help me find a school for him?'

Mr Wickfield thought for a moment. 'There's a very good school I can recommend, Dr Strong's, but the boy can't board there, and it's too far to travel from Dover every day. However, he could live here, if you liked, in my house. There's plenty of room for him.'

'That's very kind of you, Mr Wickfield. I'll pay you for his food, of course,' said my aunt.

'Come and meet Agnes, who takes care of everything and manages the house,' said Mr Wickfield. We all went upstairs to another sitting-room, prettily furnished, where a girl of my own age was sitting. On her face I saw immediately the beautiful, calm expression of the lady in the painting downstairs, and I knew she must be Mr Wickfield's daughter, Agnes. When I saw the way Mr Wickfield looked at Agnes and held her hand, I realized that she was the only thing that made life worth living for him. The lady in the painting was her mother, who had died some years before, and Agnes was now in complete charge of the house. She welcomed me warmly as a guest, and showed me the comfortable bedroom I would sleep in. My aunt was very happy to leave me in the care of Mr Wickfield and his daughter.

'I must leave now, David,' she told me. 'Mr Wickfield will take you to school tomorrow, and make all the arrangements. I'm sure you will work hard, and do well.'

'Thank you, aunt!' I said, trying not to cry. 'And give my love to Mr Dick! And thank you again!'

When she had gone, I dried my tears and spent a pleasant evening with the Wickfields. We ate supper and talked in the pretty little sitting-room. Agnes played the piano and tried to amuse her father, but he often looked serious and rather sad. During the evening he drank a good deal of wine. I wondered why he seemed unhappy.

The next day I had my first experience of a well-organized school. It could not have been more different from Salem House. The headmaster, Dr Strong, was a gentle, kind man who enjoyed teaching and never punished anybody. I soon made friends with the other boys, and as time went on, with the teachers too. But although I liked school very much, I was always happy to return to the Wickfields' quiet house every evening. There, Agnes used to help me with my studies and listen sympathetically to my problems, and her father always seemed pleased to see me. I often wrote to my aunt and Peggotty, and Mr Dick came to visit me once a week.

The strangest person in my new life was Uriah Heep. Soon after I arrived in Canterbury, we had a conversation one evening. He was doing a lot of Mr Wickfield's work, and was working late in his small office, just off the hall of the Wickfields' house.

'Come in, come in, Master Copperfield!' he cried when he saw me passing the door. I entered, and found him reading a large dusty book, and making careful notes in a notebook.

'What are you studying, Uriah?' I asked politely.

'I'm going to be a lawyer,' he replied, rubbing his thin hands together and smiling his oily smile.

'You're Mr Wickfield's assistant, aren't you? Perhaps one day you'll be his partner,' I said, trying to make conversation.

'Oh no, Master Copperfield!' cried Uriah, rolling his eyes upwards. 'I could never rise so high! No, I'm much too humble for that! But thank you, Master Copperfield, for thinking kindly of me. And may I say, that if ever you have the time (and I'm sure

'*I could never rise so high! No,
I'm much too humble for that!*'

a young gentleman like you is much too busy to spare the time for a poor person like me), my mother and I would be glad to offer you a cup of tea at our humble home.'

'Of course – if I have time,' I answered, and left the room quickly. I did not feel comfortable with him, for some reason.

But the following week he invited me to tea again, and I did not want to appear rude, so I agreed. That evening he and I walked to the small house where he lived with his mother. It was a warm day and we were drinking our tea near the open door when a gentleman I recognized passed by. It was Mr Micawber! He saw me sitting near the door and called out, 'Copperfield! Is it really you?'

I was delighted to see him again, and Mrs Heep invited him in for some tea. I had to introduce him to the Heeps, but I did not think that Uriah would be a good influence on Mr Micawber. However, I was interested to discover that the Micawbers were now living in Canterbury, as nothing had 'turned up' in Devon. They seemed to be very short of money again, and surrounded by creditors as usual. I left the Heeps' house as soon as possible, taking Mr Micawber with me, as I did not want him to tell Uriah all about my life at the warehouse in London.

And so the years passed. I learnt everything that Dr Strong and his teachers could teach me, and at seventeen, came to the end of my schooldays. My aunt suggested that, before deciding what profession to choose, I should spend a month in London or travelling round the country. This would give me time to consider my next step. I agreed enthusiastically, and although I was sorry to say goodbye to my sweet friend Agnes and her father, I was looking forward to leading the life of an independent young gentleman.

David meets old friends again

I decided to go to London first, to stay at a hotel for a few nights, and see all the sights of that great city. I knew it would be very different from the last time I was in London, when I was working at the warehouse. Now I was adult, and educated, and had money.

The hotel I chose was called the Golden Cross, and because I looked so young, I was given a very small, dark room in the roof. But I did not feel confident enough to complain.

That evening I was returning from the theatre when I recognized someone going into the hotel. I could not prevent myself from saying at once, 'Steerforth! Do you remember me?'

He stared at me for a moment. Then he cried, 'Good heavens! It's little Copperfield!'

I was so delighted to see him that I held both his hands, saying, 'My dear Steerforth, you have no idea how pleased I am to see you again!' I remembered how much I had admired him, and all my love for him came back. I had to brush away the tears from my eyes.

'Don't cry, Copperfield, old boy!' he said kindly. 'I'm glad to see you too. What are you doing here?'

'I've just finished school, and my aunt has sent me to London to look around before deciding on a profession. What about you, Steerforth?'

'Well, I'm studying at Oxford University, but nothing exciting ever happens there! That's why I'm in London for a few days. But it's boring here too, isn't it?'

'In London?' I asked, surprised. 'I think it's wonderful! There's so much to do and see! I've just been to the theatre – the actors were excellent and—'

'David, David!' laughed Steerforth. 'It does me good to see your fresh, innocent face, so full of excitement! Now, let me see, which room are you staying in?'

'Number 44. It's rather high up,' I confessed, blushing.

'They've put you in number 44? I'll soon change that.' And when Steerforth complained to the manager, I was immediately given a large, airy, comfortable room on the first floor, next to his. That night as I fell asleep I thought happily of the next few days, which Steerforth and I were planning to spend together.

A week passed very quickly, with visits to the theatre, the museums and the zoo. We went sightseeing, riding, swimming and boating. Steerforth was the perfect companion to have, and I admired him even more than before. In fact, I loved him with all my heart.

One day I said to him, 'You know, Steerforth, I really must go and visit my mother's old servant, Peggotty. She was very good to me when I was a child.'

'Yes, David, I remember you told me. She lives in Yarmouth now, doesn't she? Why don't we go there together?'

'Oh yes, Steerforth! You'd enjoy meeting her brother, and all the family! They're very kind, good people.'

'Even if they *are* only working people,' said Steerforth. I looked quickly at him to see what he meant, but he was smiling at me, so I knew he was joking, and I smiled too.

We travelled to Yarmouth by coach, and when we arrived, Steerforth stayed at the hotel while I went to Barkis's house to find Peggotty. When I knocked at the door, Peggotty opened it, and did not recognize me for a moment. I had continued to write to her regularly, but we had not seen each other for seven years, and I was no longer the small boy she remembered. But when she realized I was her Master David, she sobbed and sobbed with delight, holding me in her arms as she had always done. Soon she was calmer, and we talked about the events of the last few years. I heard that she was very happy with Mr Barkis, who, however, was ill in bed at the time. She was so pleased to see me that she insisted I should sleep at her house during my stay in Yarmouth, in the little bedroom she had always kept for me.

The next day I took Steerforth with me to visit Daniel Peggotty. It was a dark and windy winter evening. As we came closer to the old boat, we heard happy voices and laughter inside. I opened the door, and suddenly I was surrounded by Daniel, Ham and Emily, all looking very surprised.

'Look! It's Master David! Look how he's grown!'

And for a moment we were all shaking hands and talking and laughing at the same time. I did not forget to introduce Steerforth. They welcomed him warmly as my best friend.

'Well!' cried Daniel Peggotty, his large face red and shining with delight. 'It's wonderful, Master David, that you two gentlemen have come here tonight of all nights! The best night of my life! Because tonight, gentlemen, my little Emily –' and he took Emily's small white hand in his rough red one and placed it on his heart – 'has agreed to become Ham's wife!'

'I congratulate you with all my heart,' said Steerforth politely to Ham, without taking his eyes off Emily, who was blushing prettily.

'Master David knows how I love this girl,' continued old Daniel, 'and my dearest wish was for her to have a good husband to take care of her. And there's no one I trust more than Ham! He's only a rough sailor like me, but he's honest, and sincere, and I know she'll come to no harm while he lives!'

Meanwhile, Ham was blushing too. I did not know what to say, unsure whether I still loved Emily and was therefore jealous of Ham, or whether I was glad they were going to be happy together. But Steerforth always knew the right thing to say, and with a few well-chosen words he made us all feel much more comfortable.

We spent the rest of the evening very pleasantly, telling stories and singing songs, and it was midnight when Steerforth and I left the old boat.

'Well!' said Steerforth to me as we walked across the sand in the cold night air. 'What a lovely girl! And what a coarse young man she's engaged to!'

I was shocked by these unexpectedly cold words. But when I turned to him and saw him smiling, I replied warmly, 'Ah, Steerforth! You pretend to laugh at people who are poorer or less educated than yourself, but I've just seen you spend the whole evening with the Peggotty family, making them happy! I know you understand and love them, and I admire you all the more for it!'

He stopped and looked at me, saying rather sadly, 'David, you're serious, aren't you? I wish I were as good as you!'

For the next two weeks I was often with Peggotty and Barkis, while Steerforth went sailing or fishing with Daniel and Ham, or found other things to do, so I did not see very much of him. Finally we decided to return to London.

While we were travelling back on the coach, I turned to say something, and was surprised to see how miserable he looked.

'Oh David!' he said unhappily. 'I wish I could control myself better! I hate myself sometimes!'

'Steerforth! What can you mean!' I cried. 'You're the best, the most intelligent, the kindest of men!'

'Thank you, David,' he said, shaking his head, 'but you don't know how bad I am.'

'Bad!' I repeated. 'My dear Steerforth! Don't say that! I know your character well, and I'm proud to call you my friend!'

In a little while his mood changed, and he became cheerful again. I soon forgot his words, but I remembered them later.

In London I discovered that my aunt had arrived at the Golden Cross Hotel, and had booked a room there for several days. We were delighted to see each other, and had a long conversation that evening. She had come to ask me a particular question.

'David,' she said very seriously, 'I've been thinking about your future profession. How would you feel about becoming a lawyer?'

I thought for a moment. 'Well, aunt, it sounds a very good idea. I confess I hadn't considered it before, but I think I'd like it.'

'Very good,' said my aunt, jumping up. 'In that case, let's go immediately to see Mr Spenlow. He's a partner in an important law firm, and I think he'll agree to train you. We'll have to pay him, of course, but after several years you'll be a properly trained lawyer, and be able to earn your own money.'

And so we carried out this plan. My aunt paid Mr Spenlow's firm a thousand pounds, and I promised to work hard and do my best to become a successful lawyer. Before she returned to Dover, my aunt rented a small flat for me, at the top of a house near the lawcourts, and I moved in at once.

At first it seemed very exciting to walk through the busy streets after a long day in the courts or at Mr Spenlow's dusty office, and know that I had my own home to return to. But when I had climbed up all the stairs, and entered my sitting-room, it no longer seemed so exciting. In fact, my flat looked empty and depressing. So, after two days of loneliness, I was very glad to receive my first visitor, Steerforth, and because I was so happy to see him, I invited him and two friends of his to dinner the next evening.

As it was my first dinner party, I did not know what to buy, but I ordered cooked dishes of chicken and fish from the restaurant, bought cheese and fruit from the market, and had a large number of bottles of wine delivered. I was quite frightened by how much money I had spent, but when Steerforth and his friends arrived, I soon became more cheerful. The party was a great success, and we all enjoyed ourselves very much. We ate, and drank, and smoked, and drank again. I was constantly opening bottles of wine, and became unusually talkative. I began to feel rather strange, and when I caught sight of myself in a mirror, I seemed very pale. I had to confess to myself that I looked drunk.

Someone suggested going to the theatre, and in a kind of mist we left my flat and walked through the streets. Steerforth was holding my arm and laughing. Then a man in a little box looked out of the fog, and took money from somebody. Soon we were sitting high up in a very hot, very crowded theatre. There were bright lights, and there was music, but I could not understand what anyone was saying, and the whole building seemed to swim in front of my eyes.

Then someone suggested going to visit some friends in another part of the theatre, so we went downstairs. Suddenly I saw, quite clearly, Agnes Wickfield, sitting with a lady and gentleman. She was looking at me with a surprised expression on her face.

'Good heavens!' I cried. 'Agnes! You're in London!'

'Quiet!' she whispered. 'People are trying to listen to the actors. You'll disturb them!' Then she added kindly, 'David, please do what I say. Ask your friends to take you home.'

I had always taken Agnes's advice, and I did so this time. I do not remember how I got home, but I do remember Steerforth helping me to undress and get into bed. What a terrible, sleepless night I spent! How ill I felt! How dry my mouth was! But the next morning I felt even worse. I was so miserable and ashamed that I had been so stupid, and that Agnes had seen me drunk. I could not even apologize to her, because I did not know where she was staying in London. I spent the whole day with my head in my hands, in my dirty, smoky room, surrounded by empty wine bottles.

But the next day a note was delivered to my flat. It was from Agnes, asking me to visit her at the house where she was staying. I went straight there after my day's work at the office.

She looked so quiet and good, and reminded me so much of my happy schooldays in Canterbury, that I could not help crying.

'I'm so sorry, Agnes,' I said, 'that you saw me like that. I wish I were dead!'

'David, don't be unhappy,' she said cheerfully. 'You know you can trust me, and I'll always be your friend.'

I took her hand and kissed it. 'Agnes, you're my good angel!'

She shook her head. 'No, David, but if I were, I'd warn you – to stay away from your bad angel.'

'My dear Agnes!' I cried. 'Do you mean Steerforth?'

'I do, David,' she replied, looking firmly at me.

'Agnes, you're wrong! He is my trusted friend! He helps and guides me! It wasn't his fault that I got drunk, you know!'

'I wasn't thinking of that. I judge him from what you've told me about him, and your character, and his influence over you.' Agnes spoke very seriously, and her words went straight to my heart. 'I'm certain I'm right. You've made a dangerous friend,

David, because you're so trusting. Please remember what I say – and forgive me for saying it.'

'I will, if *you* forgive *me* for getting drunk.'

Agnes agreed, smiling, and then said suddenly, 'Have you seen Uriah Heep?'

'No,' I replied. 'Is he in London? What's he doing here?'

'I'm worried, David,' answered Agnes with sadness in her beautiful eyes. 'I think he's going to be Father's partner.'

I remembered Uriah Heep's oily smile, and how uncomfortable he always used to make me feel.

'What? That creature? He's so unpleasant! You must prevent your father from agreeing to it, Agnes!'

Agnes smiled miserably. 'My poor father has no choice. You know how unhappy he has often been? And of course you've seen him drinking. You see, he loved my mother very much, and when she died, he didn't care so much about his work. That's when he started drinking. Uriah's very clever – he knows all this, and he's been very useful to Father, doing all the work that Father had forgotten or didn't want to do. Father really needs Uriah now, to keep his business going. And Uriah himself pretends to be humble and grateful, but in fact he's in a strong position, and is insisting on becoming a partner. Father is ashamed of himself, but he has to agree. Poor Father! I'd do anything to help him, anything!' And Agnes sobbed bitterly.

I had never seen Agnes cry before. It made me so sad that I could only say helplessly, 'My dear Agnes! Please don't cry!' However, in a few minutes she was calm again, and I was able to leave her, promising to visit her and her father in Canterbury very soon.

'Poor Father! I'd do anything
to help him, anything!'

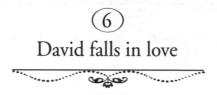

6
David falls in love

Agnes had asked me to be polite to Uriah if I met him, and so, when I saw him the next day near the lawcourts, I was careful not to offend him. He looked even stranger than before, with his small evil head and long thin body, and his wide oily smile. When we shook hands, I noticed how cold and wet his hand felt, just like a fish.

'Would you – would you like to come to my rooms for coffee, Uriah?' I offered, trying to hide my horror of him.

'Oh, Master Copperfield, I mean, *Mister* Copperfield, I should say now! How kind of you! I'm too humble to expect such kindness! But I *would* like that!'

And when we reached my flat, he looked at me with an unpleasantly confident smile, and said, 'Perhaps you've heard that I'm going to become Mr Wickfield's partner, Mr Copperfield?'

'Yes,' I replied. 'Agnes has told me about it.'

'Ah! I'm glad to hear that Miss Agnes knows about it,' he answered. 'Thank you for that, Mr Copperfield!'

I was annoyed with myself for mentioning Agnes's name, and hated hearing him say it, but I said nothing and drank my coffee.

'You said once, Mr Copperfield,' continued Uriah, rubbing his hands together happily, 'that perhaps I'd be Mr Wickfield's partner one day. It was kind of you to say so. A humble person like me remembers things like that! And now it's true! I'm glad to think I've been able to help poor Mr Wickfield. Oh, how very careless he has been! If I hadn't been his assistant, he would certainly have lost his business, his house, and all his money by now. Of course,

I'm helping him because I admire him – and not only him . . .'

Suddenly, although the room was warm, an icy coldness spread through my body, as I stared into his cruel little face.

'Miss Agnes is looking beautiful at the moment, isn't she?' he went on, smiling horribly. 'Mr Copperfield, I trust you, because as you know, I've always liked you, although I'm so humble, and you're a gentleman. So I'd like to tell you my little secret. In spite of my low position, I love Miss Agnes! I've given my heart to her, and I hope to marry her one day!'

There was a purple mist in front of my eyes. I wanted to hit his ugly face, or stab a knife right into his wicked heart. I was almost mad with anger. But I thought of Agnes's request, and I managed to control myself.

'Have – have you spoken to Agnes about your – your love?' I asked as calmly as I could.

'Oh no, Mr Copperfield. I'm waiting for the right moment. Perhaps I'll ask her when I become her father's partner. She'll think kindly of me, you see, when she realizes how much her father needs me. She loves him so much! Ah, what a good daughter my Agnes is! And what an excellent wife she'll be to me!'

Dear, sweet Agnes, my adopted sister! I did not know any man good enough to be her husband. Could she ever marry this worthless insect? When Uriah left my flat, I spent a sleepless night worrying about what I should do. In the end I decided to say nothing to Agnes about Uriah's plan, as she already had enough to worry about.

A year had passed since I first started work in Mr Spenlow's firm. I often went to court with him, and began to understand the details of some of the most difficult cases. Mr Spenlow was kind to me, and occasionally talked to me, not only about law but also about other matters. I discovered that his wife had died, and that he lived in a large country house just outside London, with his only daughter and her paid companion. One day he invited me to his house for the weekend, and I accepted gratefully. So on Friday evening Mr Spenlow's coach and horses drove us to the house.

When I saw the Spenlows' home, I realized how rich Mr Spenlow must be. It was a lovely old building, with large gardens. As soon as we entered, Mr Spenlow asked one of the servants, 'Where's Miss Dora?'

'Dora!' I thought. 'What a beautiful name!' We went into the sitting-room, and I suppose Mr Spenlow introduced me. I did not notice, because nothing mattered at that moment. I just stared stupidly at his daughter Dora, lost in wonder at her beauty, and unable to say anything. I had fallen in love in a second.

As I stared, I heard a voice speaking to me, but it was not Dora's. It was her companion, whom I had not noticed at all while Mr Spenlow was making the introductions. When I saw that the companion was Miss Murdstone, I was surprised, certainly, but nothing could take my attention away from Dora for more than a second or two.

Mr Spenlow explained that Miss Murdstone had been kind enough to come and look after his poor motherless daughter, and to be her confidential friend and companion. But it seemed to me that Dora was neither friendly nor confidential towards her stern companion.

As for me, the rest of the weekend passed in a kind of fog. We ate meals, and went for walks. People spoke to me, and I answered. But I have no idea what I actually said. All I remember was Dora's golden hair, and Dora's blushing face, and Dora's beautiful blue eyes! Occasionally I was lucky enough to speak to her alone, and then I was so shy that I blushed as much as Dora herself. I was very jealous of the little dog that she carried everywhere with her. Sometimes I thought she liked me a little, and at other times I was sure she would never love me. I was wildly, desperately in love!

I had wondered if Miss Murdstone would try and blacken my name with the Spenlows, but on that first evening she had taken me to one side.

'David Copperfield,' she said coldly. 'I see no need for either of us to speak about the past to anyone here. I imagine we are agreed on that.'

'Certainly, ma'am. We are agreed on that, although I shall never change my opinion of you.'

I put Miss Murdstone out of my mind, and for several weeks after meeting Dora, I lived in a dream. I did my work automatically, and I never stopped thinking of her. The greatest happiness I could imagine was being engaged to Dora. I dared not hope that one day we would be married.

While walking round London one day, hoping to meet Dora out shopping, I met my old schoolfriend Tommy Traddles. He was living in the city, like me, and was also studying to become a lawyer. I arranged to visit him, and went to his house after work the next day. He lived in one room in a rented house, in a very poor part of the city. His room was small, and almost empty.

'Copperfield! I'm glad to see you!' he said warmly. 'You can see I haven't got much furniture, but I'm hoping to earn more money later, when I've finished my studies.'

'Didn't you have a rich uncle, Traddles?' I asked.

'Yes, but I've always been unlucky, you know. He decided he didn't like me, so he didn't leave me anything when he died. I'm really very poor, and I have to do several jobs to pay for my studies.' Traddles looked surprisingly cheerful. 'But I must tell you, Copperfield, as you're an old friend, that I'm engaged! To a lovely girl, who comes from a large family, and lives in Devon!'

I was thinking of Dora as I shook hands with him and congratulated him enthusiastically. 'Will you get married soon?' I asked.

'No, she's very poor too, so we'll have to wait a long time, until we've saved enough money. She's such a dear girl, Copperfield. She says she'll wait for me until she's sixty, if necessary! And I'm quite happy here with the people who rent the house – the Micawbers are very kind.'

'Who did you say?' I cried. 'The Micawbers! I know them!'

Just then Mr Micawber himself knocked at the door and entered. His stomach was a little fatter and his face a little older than before, but he looked as confident as ever. I went up to him and shook his hand.

'How are you, Mr Micawber?' I asked. 'Do you remember me?'

'Is it possible? Can it be? Have I the pleasure of seeing my old friend Copperfield again?' he replied, a smile spreading over his large face. He turned to call downstairs, 'My dear! Come and meet this gentleman, my love!'

When Mrs Micawber came in, she was also delighted to see me, and we talked for some time about the twins, and the other children, and her husband's business interests. But this conversation soon made Mr Micawber rather depressed.

'You see, Copperfield,' he said miserably, 'nothing has turned up yet. Sometimes I wonder whether anything ever *will* turn up. I can't pay for our food, or even our water. It's hard enough for *me* to accept the situation, but how can I expect my dear wife to live like this? Perhaps it would have been better if I had never asked her to marry me!' He put his head in his hands.

'Micawber!' cried his wife. 'How can you say that! You know I have always loved and admired you, and always will love and admire you! My dear husband!' And they fell into each other's arms, sobbing on each other's shoulders. In a few moments they had both dried their eyes and looked quite cheerful again. I realized that the Micawbers had not changed at all, but this quick change of mood was rather a surprise for Traddles.

Before I left, I made sure I had a word in private with my old schoolfriend. 'Traddles,' I whispered, 'take my advice – don't lend Mr Micawber any money. He's got a lot of debts.'

Traddles looked uncomfortable. 'Thank you, Copperfield,' he whispered in reply, 'but I've already lent him some. I don't know whether he'll give it back – you know how unlucky I am!'

When I got back to my rooms, I found Steerforth waiting for me there. I thought of Agnes's warning about him, but when I saw his open, good-looking face, I could not believe he could be a bad influence on anyone. However, there was something rather strange in his manner that night. Sometimes he seemed quite depressed, almost desperate, but a minute later he was laughing wildly, and I had no idea why he was like that.

'I've just been to Yarmouth, David!' he told me.

'Oh!' I replied. 'You've seen the Peggotty family, I expect?'

'I haven't seen much of them, but I *have* got some news for you. It's about old Barkis. I'm afraid his illness has got much worse, and the doctor thinks he'll die very soon.'

'Oh dear!' I said. 'Poor Peggotty will be so sad!'

'Yes, it's bad luck,' replied Steerforth carelessly. 'But people die in this world every minute. I'm not afraid of death! I want to live life in my own way, and nobody can stop me!' He threw his head back proudly. I looked into his handsome face, wondering why he was so excited, which was unusual for him.

'Steerforth, I think I'll have to go to Yarmouth myself,' I said. 'Perhaps I can help Peggotty at this difficult time.'

Smiling, he put his hands on my shoulders. 'I wish I could be as good as you! David, promise me that if anything ever happens to separate us, you'll think of me at my best! Promise me that!'

'Steerforth, you have no best or worst for me,' I answered. 'You will always have your place in my heart!'

And as he turned to go, he gave me his hand, and smiled in his old friendly way. That is how I like to remember him, now that I shall never touch his hand again, or see him smile.

When I arrived in Yarmouth, I went straight to Barkis's house. In the sitting-room I found Daniel, Ham and Emily. Ham was standing by the door, while Emily was sobbing in Daniel's arms. None of them seemed surprised to see me.

'Emily's very young, Master David,' explained Daniel. 'It's hard for her to accept death. That's why she's crying. Now cheer up, Emily my dear, Ham has come to take you home. What's that?' He bent his grey head down to hear her whispered reply. 'You want to stay here with your old uncle? But you should go with Ham – he'll be your husband soon!'

'That's all right,' said Ham. 'If it makes Emily happy, it'll make me happy. I'll go home alone.' He went over to Emily and gave her a gentle kiss. She seemed to turn away from him a little. As Ham went out, I went upstairs to see poor Barkis.

He was lying unconscious in bed, looking very pale and ill. Peggotty was sitting beside him. She jumped up and took me delightedly in her arms, just as she used to do. Then she turned to her husband. 'Barkis, my dear,' she said almost cheerfully, 'here's Master David, who brought us together, you remember? He carried your messages for you. Can you speak to him?'

Barkis lay silently there, not moving. We sat beside him all through that long night. In the early morning, he suddenly opened his eyes, reached out his hand to me, and said clearly, with a pleasant smile, 'Barkis is willing!' And then he closed his eyes, and died.

'He was a good man!' said Peggotty, with tears in her eyes. 'I shall miss him!'

I was able to help Peggotty with the arrangements for the funeral. Barkis was buried in Blunderstone churchyard, close to my mother and little brother. We discovered that Barkis had saved quite a lot of money, which he left to Peggotty and Daniel. So I knew that Peggotty would not need to work in future.

On the day before the funeral, we all arranged to meet at the old boat. It was my last evening in Yarmouth, as I was returning to London the following day. When I arrived, I was surprised to see that Ham and Emily were not there. Peggotty was feeling more cheerful now, and Daniel was talking to her. Just then Ham came to the door.

'Master David, come outside a minute, would you?' he asked. I stepped outside, and Ham shut the door carefully. It was raining heavily, and as we stood on the lonely beach, I noticed how very pale Ham's face was.

'Ham!' I cried. 'What's the matter?'

'Master David!' he sobbed wildly. I had never seen such a strong man cry like that before. 'It's Emily! I'd have died for her! I love her with all my heart! But she's run away and – worse than that! Oh, how I wish God had saved her from this ruin!'

I shall never forget his desperate face turned towards me, and the pain in his honest eyes.

'You're educated, Master David!' he continued. 'You know how to express yourself! Help me! How can I ever explain to *him* in there? He loves her even more than I do!'

I saw the door open, and tried to stop Ham speaking, but it was too late. Daniel Peggotty came out, and when he saw us, he seemed to realize immediately what we were talking about. The expression on his face changed in a moment, and he pulled us both back inside. I found myself with a letter in my hand which Ham had given me.

'Read it, sir,' said Daniel, his face pale and trembling and his eyes wild. 'Read it slowly, please.'

The room was completely silent as I read aloud:

Dear Ham,
Please, please, forgive me for running away and leaving you. When you see this, I'll be far away. I shall never return to my dear home unless he marries me and brings me back as a lady. Oh, I'm so sorry, and so ashamed! I know this will break your heart, but believe me, I'm not good enough for you! I'm too wicked. Tell Uncle I'll always love him, even if he can never love me again. And I'll always think of you, dear Ham, even if you hate me for what I've done. Forgive me, and goodbye!
Emily

Daniel did not move for a long time after I had finished reading. I took his hand, but he did not notice. Suddenly he appeared to wake up, and said in a low voice,

'Who's the man? I want to know his name.'

Ham looked quickly at me, and I felt a shock run through my whole body. I fell on to a chair and could not speak.

'Don't listen, Master David,' Ham said, hesitating, 'we don't blame you for it.' Peggotty put her arm round my neck, but I could not move. 'A – gentleman's been here very often recently,' continued Ham in a broken voice, 'and – today people saw Emily driving off with him in his coach!'

'Tell me!' cried Daniel wildly. 'Is his name Steerforth?'

'It is!' replied Ham just as wildly, 'and I'm sorry, Master David, but he's the wickedest man I've ever known!'

After a moment Daniel spoke. He looked suddenly much older. 'I wish I'd drowned him when I had the chance! But it's too late now. There's no peace for me here while my dear girl is away. I'm going to look for her, and bring her back home. Don't any of you try to stop me! Ham, you must stay here in Yarmouth. Keep a light always burning in the window of this house, so that if the poor girl ever comes back, she can find her way home across the sand. I'm going to London, and France, and all over the world if necessary. I'm prepared to spend my whole life travelling until I find her. If anything happens to me, if I don't come back, tell her I forgive her – tell her my love for her is unchanged!'

And although we all tried hard to persuade him to stay, he refused to listen. He took his coat, hat, bag and stick, and stepped out into the darkness. We watched him walking along the London road, until he disappeared from sight. I often thought of that lonely figure in the next few weeks and months, walking through strange streets in foreign cities, looking for his adopted child. When I thought of him, I remembered his last words to us: *If anything happens to me, if I don't come back, tell her I forgive her – tell her my love for her is unchanged!*

He took his coat, hat, bag and stick,
and stepped out into the darkness.

7

Good news and bad news for David

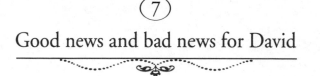

All this time I had gone on loving Dora more than ever. The more evil there seemed to be in the world, the more brightly Dora's star shone down on me. I am sure I considered her a beautiful angel, far above the rest of us poor humans, and I had no real hope of persuading her to love me.

Peggotty had come to London with me, as she was feeling rather lonely after Barkis's death and Daniel's departure, and I could not stop myself telling her all about Dora. She was very interested, and most encouraging.

'The young lady should be very proud to have such a handsome, intelligent young man as you, Master David!' she cried. 'And I'm sure her father will be delighted to accept you as her husband!' But I could not share her hopeful view of the situation.

However, a wonderful thing happened. During a long conversation with Mr Spenlow in the office, he mentioned that it was Dora's birthday the following week, and invited me to a picnic to celebrate it. As soon as I heard this, I went completely mad, and could not think at all clearly. In the next week I bought expensive new clothes and boots, and arranged to hire a handsome white horse. On the day of the picnic, I got up at six in the morning and went to Covent Garden market to buy the freshest and most beautiful flowers for Dora, and by ten o'clock I was riding towards the Spenlows' house.

How lovely Dora looked, in her sky-blue dress and white hat, when I met her in the garden in front of the house! And when she accepted my flowers with delight, I almost thought I would die of happiness.

'You'll be glad to hear, Mr Copperfield,' she said, smiling prettily, 'that cross Miss Murdstone isn't here. She'll be away for at least three weeks. Instead I have my dear friend, Miss Julia Mills, here with me.'

Sitting next to Dora was a young lady I had not noticed before. Although she was only about twenty, she looked very calm and wise. I later discovered that she had had an unhappy experience in love, and had decided never again to become personally involved in matters of the heart.

'How delightful for you!' I answered, blushing as I always did when I spoke to Dora. 'And everything that is delightful to *you* is delightful to *me*, Miss Spenlow!' Miss Mills said nothing, but smiled kindly on us both.

To get to the picnic place, which was some way from the house, Mr Spenlow, Dora and Miss Mills drove in an open carriage, while I rode by their side on my handsome white horse. I shall never have such a ride again. Dora sat with her back to the horses, looking towards me, and holding my flowers close to her sweet face. Our eyes often met, and I am surprised I did not fall off my horse. I did not notice the dust, or the road we were taking. Sometimes Mr Spenlow spoke to me about the scenery, and I replied politely, but I cannot remember what I said. All I could see was Dora.

I was very disappointed when we arrived, to find that other guests had been invited. I was quite jealous even of the ladies, because they talked to Dora and took her away from me, but I *hated* all the men as soon as I saw them. There was a very unpleasant, talkative man with a red moustache, who insisted he knew all about preparing food, and soon had most of the young ladies round him. One of them was Dora. I felt that he was now my worst enemy.

When we started eating, I saw to my horror that Red Moustache was sitting, with a huge plate of chicken, at Dora's feet! I could not think clearly, but I pretended to be cheerful. I sat with a young lady dressed in pink, and talked amusingly to her, and looked at her, and fetched her whatever she needed. Sometimes I looked over at Dora, and she looked back at me, but she had Red Moustache and I had the young lady in pink.

After the meal, the young lady's mother took her away, and I walked alone into a wood, feeling angry and desperate. I was just planning to ride away on my handsome white horse, although I did not know where to, when I saw Dora and Miss Mills coming to meet me.

'Mr Copperfield,' said Miss Mills, 'you are unhappy.'

'No, no, Miss Mills!' I protested firmly. 'Perfectly happy!'

'And Dora,' continued Miss Mills, 'you are unhappy.'

'Oh good heavens, no, Julia!' cried Dora. 'Not at all!'

'Mr Copperfield and Dora,' said Miss Mills, looking old and wise, 'enough of this foolishness! You love each other! Confess it and be happy! Take the chance that life offers you! Listen to one who speaks from bitter experience!'

I was so hot and excited that I took Dora's little hand immediately and kissed it – and she let me! I kissed Miss Mills's hand too, and life seemed wonderful again.

Dora shyly put her arm in mine and we walked about together, until, much too soon, we heard the other guests calling her name. So we had to go back, and when they wanted Dora to sing a song, Red Moustache offered to fetch the guitar from the carriage for her. But Dora told him nobody except me knew where it was.

So I fetched the guitar, and I held her gloves, and I sat beside her while she sang. And I knew that in that great crowd of people she was singing only for me, who loved her.

When the guests left, I rode beside the carriage all the way back to the Spenlows' house. Mr Spenlow, who had drunk a lot of wine, was asleep in his seat, and Miss Mills was smiling in a motherly way, as Dora and I whispered happily to each other. Once Miss Mills called me to her side of the carriage.

'Dora is coming to stay with me,' she told me quietly, 'the day after tomorrow. Perhaps you would like to visit us?'

'Miss Mills! How can I ever thank you?' I said. 'What a friend you are – to Miss Spenlow and me!'

When we arrived at the Spenlows' house, I had to say goodbye to Dora and ride back to London. On the way, I remembered everything she had done or said ten thousand times. I decided I had to tell her I loved her as soon as possible, and ask whether she loved me too. It was the most important question in the world, and only Dora could give me the answer to it.

So, two days later, I dressed in my finest clothes and went to the address Miss Mills had given me. The servant took me to the sitting-room, where I found Julia Mills learning a song, and Dora painting the flowers I had given her! After a short conversation Miss Mills made an excuse and left the room, and Dora and I were alone together.

'I hope your poor horse wasn't tired the other night,' said Dora, raising her beautiful eyes to mine. 'It was a long way for him, to and from the picnic place.'

I must ask her today! I thought. My whole body was trembling. 'It was a long way for *him*,' I answered. 'For me it seemed very short, because of my happiness in being so near you.'

Dora and I whispered happily to each other.

There was a moment's silence. Then Dora said, 'You didn't seem to care for that happiness earlier in the day, when you were sitting with the lady in pink. But I expect you don't mean what you say. And of course you're quite free to do whatever you like!'

I don't know how I did it. It happened so quickly. Suddenly I had Dora in my arms and I couldn't stop speaking. I told her how I loved her. I told her I would die without her. And when she blushed and cried a little, I said I had loved her day and night since the moment I had first seen her. I told her that nobody had ever loved or could ever love as much as I loved her.

Somehow I found myself sitting quietly next to Dora on the sofa, holding her little hand. We were engaged! I suppose we realized that one day we would get married, but for the moment we were going to keep our engagement secret from Mr Spenlow. When Miss Mills came in, she was delighted to hear our news, and promised to help us as much as possible.

Now began one of the happiest times of my life. When I look back, I see how foolish I was, but how loving and sincere! I visited Dora every day, and I did not have time for anyone or anything else. But in the middle of my excitement I suddenly thought of Agnes, of her clear calm eyes and her gentle face, and I sat down immediately to write to her, and tell her all about Dora. I knew that as my adopted sister she would share my happiness, and I wanted her approval.

One day when Peggotty and I were having tea in my flat, Tommy Traddles came to visit me. 'My dear Copperfield!' he cried. 'I've been several times before, but you've been out.'

'My dear Traddles,' I replied, 'yes, I'm very sorry, I've been visiting my – Miss D, you know.'

'I expect she lives in London, doesn't she? Mine – that's Sophy
– beautiful name, isn't it? Mine lives in Devon, I think I told you.
So I don't see her very often. She really is the dearest girl! She's
very busy at home, you know, looking after the other nine children.
And her mother, who's unable to walk.'

'What a wonderful girl she must be!' I agreed politely. 'And
tell me, Traddles, how is Mr Micawber?'

'I'm not living in his house at the moment,' said Traddles, 'because
his creditors demanded payment of his debts recently, and he had
to move to another house. To avoid these unpleasant men, he's
even changed his name to Mortimer, and he only comes out of
the house after dark, wearing glasses.'

'So nothing has turned up for him yet? And what about the
money you lent him, Traddles?'

'I'm afraid I may not get it back. But Mr Micawber promises
to give it back one day. He's a fine, honest man, isn't he?' And
Traddles looked hopefully at me.

Before I could reply, we heard footsteps on the stairs. I was
very surprised to see my aunt coming upstairs. She was carrying
two cases and her cat, and was followed closely by Mr Dick, carrying
two more cases.

'My dear aunt!' I cried. 'What an unexpected pleasure!' We
kissed each other, and I shook hands with Mr Dick. Traddles left
quietly, as he could see we would be discussing family matters.
Peggotty made some more tea for my aunt, who had sat down
heavily on her cases.

'Dear aunt!' I said. 'Make yourself more comfortable! Sit in an
armchair, or sit on the sofa!'

'Why do you think I'm sitting on my cases?' she asked, looking
seriously at me.

I shook my head, unable to guess.

'Because what I'm sitting on is all I have! Because I've lost all my money, my dear!'

I couldn't have been more shocked if the house and all of us in it had fallen into the River Thames.

'Yes,' continued my aunt, putting her head calmly on my shoulder. 'I'll tell you all about it tomorrow, David, but tonight we must find a bed for Mr Dick, and I'll sleep here, to save money.' So that night, my aunt agreed to take my bed, while I planned to sleep on the sitting-room sofa, and I took Mr Dick to a neighbour's house to rent a room. When I returned, I found my aunt walking up and down in front of the sitting-room fire.

'That Peggotty woman is very fond of you, David!' she said. 'She's been offering to give us some of her money – the money she inherited from her husband! Of course I refused at once. But she's a good woman. And she's been telling me about the trouble at Yarmouth—'

'Yes, poor Emily!' I could not stop myself saying.

'Silly Emily, you mean! But I'm sorry for you, because you cared for her once. And now Peggotty tells me you're in love again!'

I blushed. 'I love Dora with all my heart, aunt!'

'I suppose the little thing is very lovely, is she?'

'No one can imagine how lovely she is!'

'She isn't at all silly, is she?' asked my aunt.

I had never considered this possibility before, and could only repeat what my aunt had said. 'Silly, aunt?'

'Well, well, I only ask,' replied my aunt gently. 'David, you're very loving, like your poor mother, and you need a good, serious, sensible person to love.'

'Aunt, if you only knew how sensible Dora is!' I replied.

'Oh David!' she answered. 'Blind, blind, blind!'

This made me feel a little uncomfortable, but I was glad she knew my secret. I thought perhaps she was rather tired, so I said goodnight. She went to my bedroom, and I lay down on the sofa.

How miserable I was that night! I knew I should be thinking of my poor aunt's situation, but I could not prevent myself from thinking of Dora. How could I marry her if I had no money, no expensive clothes to wear, no handsome white horse to ride or flowers to give her?

The next morning I got up early to have a walk in the fresh air, and on the way home, a carriage stopped beside me, and Agnes Wickfield got out. I immediately felt better when I saw her beautiful calm face smiling at me. She had heard that my aunt was in trouble, and had come to London to see her. We walked together to my flat.

'You know that Uriah Heep is my father's partner now?' she said quietly. 'His influence over my father is far too great. Father is much, much worse. He looks years older, and I'm afraid that, encouraged by Uriah, he drinks more than ever. Uriah and his old mother live with us now, so I can't always be with Father – to – to protect him from whatever Uriah is planning. I just hope that love and truth will always be stronger than evil!'

I could not give her my opinion of Uriah, because by then we had arrived at the flat. My aunt was very pleased to see Agnes again, and made us sit down on the sofa next to Peggotty.

'Now let me explain to you all what happened to my money,' said my aunt firmly. I was surprised to see that Agnes was pale and trembling. Betsey Trotwood continued, 'I saved a lot of money over the years, and my lawyer, Mr Wickfield, used to help me invest it in the right companies. But recently I thought he wasn't such a good lawyer as he used to be, so I decided to invest my money myself. What a lot of mistakes I made! Who knows where it's gone? In gold, and foreign banks, and so on. It's no good worrying about it, but I can tell you, there's nothing left.'

The colour was beginning to return to Agnes's face. 'So it – it wasn't my father's fault, dear Miss Trotwood?'

'Not at all, Agnes,' said my aunt cheerfully. 'Now can any of you give me some advice? I've asked my servant Janet to rent my little house in Kent. That will bring in about seventy pounds a year. I think we'll need more than that, to live on.'

'You and David could share this flat very cheaply, with Mr Dick just round the corner in his rented room,' suggested Agnes. 'And I think I can find a little job for David. Do you remember Dr Strong, the headmaster of the Canterbury school? Now that he's retired and come to live in London, he needs a private secretary to work for him in the mornings and evenings, at his house. He was asking Father about it the other day. What do you think?'

'Agnes!' I cried. 'What would we do without you? You are my good angel, I told you so before! I could easily be Dr Strong's secretary, as well as continuing my work in Mr Spenlow's firm. I'll go and see him today, and arrange it with him.'

Agnes gave me her beautiful smile as she got up to leave. I went downstairs with her, and as we walked together to the coach station, I saw an old beggar with a white stick in the street. He was holding out his thin hand for money, and crying, 'Blind! Blind! Blind!' It sounded like an echo of what my aunt had said the day before. Oh Agnes, dear sister! If I had only known then what I discovered long afterwards!

8

David's new life

With Agnes's encouragement I felt much stronger, and no longer depressed. My life now had a purpose. I intended to work as hard as I could, to help my aunt and to earn enough money to marry Dora. I got up every morning at five o'clock, walked to Dr Strong's house on the other side of London, worked with him for two hours every morning, and then walked back to Mr Spenlow's office, where I spent most of the day in the lawcourts. Then I returned to Dr Strong's for two or three more hours in the evening, and finally came home to my flat, where my aunt, Peggotty and Mr Dick would be waiting for me. I was glad to be able to tell my aunt that Dr Strong would pay me seventy pounds a year for my work. With that, and the rent from my aunt's house in Kent, we could live quite well, if we were careful. Because I was young and healthy, I did not mind hard work, and whenever I was tired, I told myself, 'You're doing it for Dora!' and that made me work even harder.

When I met Traddles one day near the courts, I told him about my new situation, and he was very sympathetic.

'But I have news for you too, Copperfield!' he said. 'The Micawbers are moving to Canterbury.'

'Oh! That means something must have turned up for them!' I replied, interested.

'Yes, Mr Micawber is going to become assistant to someone called Uriah Heep, a partner in a firm of Canterbury lawyers.'

'Heep!' I cried in horror. 'I know him! Why would Mr Micawber want to work for *him*?'

'Well, I do know that Heep has paid all Mr Micawber's debts in London,' answered Traddles. 'The whole family is leaving tomorrow. They asked me to tell you.'

I wondered why Heep wanted Micawber to work for him, and I felt sure Uriah had some evil plan in his ugly head.

. The next day Peggotty was returning to Yarmouth to look after Ham, while Daniel was away. After I had taken her to the coach station and said goodbye to her, I hurried to Miss Mills's house. I had not yet told Dora about the changes in my life, because I had not wanted to explain it all in a letter, but today she was visiting Julia Mills and was expecting me to come to tea.

How happy and beautiful Dora looked when she met me in the sitting-room! And how shocked and miserable she looked when I asked her immediately, 'Can you love a beggar, Dora?' My pretty little Dora! She had no idea what I meant.

'Don't be silly, David!' she cried. 'What *are* you talking about?'

'It's true, Dora, my love!' I cried. 'I've lost all my money! I'm a beggar!' And I looked so serious that Dora was frightened, and began to sob bitterly on my shoulder.

'But I love you, Dora, and always will!' I continued. 'It doesn't matter if we are poor, because I'll work hard to buy our bread. We don't need much as long as we have each other! Tell me your heart is still mine, dear Dora!'

'Oh yes!' she cried. 'Oh yes, it's all yours! Only, don't frighten me again! Don't talk of hard work and bread! I don't understand! I hardly ever eat bread!'

I loved her more than ever. But I felt she was not very practical. In a few moments, when she had stopped crying and was calmer, I tried again to make her understand.

'My dearest! May I mention something?'

'Oh, please don't be practical!' begged Dora, tears coming to her lovely eyes. 'It frightens me so much!'

'My dear one, if we work together, and share our problems, it will make us, and our love, stronger.'

'But I'm not strong at all!' she cried miserably. 'Ask Julia! She'll tell you – I'm weak, and foolish!'

'But if you thought sometimes, my sweet Dora, that you are engaged to a poor man – if you tried to see how your father manages the servants, or how much food costs in the markets, it would be helpful to us. We must be brave, dear Dora! Our path in life is steep and rocky—'

I was becoming quite enthusiastic, but I suddenly realized I had said far too much. Poor little Dora was sobbing and screaming with fear, and in a moment was lying unconscious on the sofa. I really thought I had killed her. I threw water on her face and went down on my knees to ask her to forgive me. I called myself a selfish, heartless creature, and shouted for Julia Mills. At last she hurried in, and I explained what had happened. When Dora opened her eyes, her friend helped her upstairs.

While Dora was upstairs, washing her face and calming herself, I asked Miss Mills's advice on the best way to encourage Dora to become more practical. Miss Mills shook her head sadly.

'I must be honest with you, Mr Copperfield. Our dearest Dora is a beautiful, innocent child of nature, full of light and happiness. She is above the things of this world, which we poor humans have to worry about. I think you'll just have to accept that fact.'

When Dora came downstairs again, she looked so lovely that I felt bitterly angry with myself for making her unhappy, even for a moment. We had tea, and she sang her French songs to me, and played the guitar. We were happy again, until the moment when

I stupidly mentioned that I had to get up at five o'clock the next morning. Suddenly her pretty face looked sad, and she did not play or sing again. When I got up to go, she came up close to me, and said lovingly, 'You bad boy, don't be so silly! Don't get up at five o'clock! Why should you?'

'But my love, I have work to do! I have to work in order to live!' I replied.

'Work? Don't be so foolish, David dear!' and she seemed to think that was the end of the matter, as she gave me a kiss straight from her innocent little heart.

I loved her, and went on loving her. But I went on working hard too, and worrying about earning money. Some evenings, as I sat opposite my aunt in my little sitting-room at the end of another exhausting day, I was quite frightened, when I thought of the problems I was going to have to solve alone.

Several months passed in this way. Dora and I wrote to each other every day, and occasionally I was able to visit her at Miss Mills's house. But one morning when I arrived at the office for work, Mr Spenlow greeted me very coldly and asked me to step into his office, where we could talk privately. When I entered the room, I was surprised to see Miss Murdstone standing by his desk, staring unpleasantly at me. I knew at once that Dora's father had discovered our secret, and I guessed who had told him.

'Mr Copperfield,' said Mr Spenlow, frowning sternly at me, 'I am sorry to say that Miss Murdstone has found some letters which appear to be from you to my daughter Dora. *Are* they yours?'

I looked at the letters he handed to me, blushed, and whispered, 'Yes, sir.' Poor little Dora! I hoped she had not been frightened by that horrible Murdstone woman. I hated to think of Dora's unhappiness at losing my letters.

'I suspected something was wrong when Miss Spenlow came back from her last visit to Miss Mills,' said Miss Murdstone, looking very pleased with herself. 'I always said Julia Mills was not a suitable friend for Miss Spenlow, and I was right!'

Mr Spenlow appeared to agree, but rather sadly.

'I am very sorry, sir,' I said, 'but it is all my fault. Please don't blame Dora—'

'Miss Spenlow to you, young man!' said her father angrily.

'I know it wasn't right to keep it secret, sir, but I love your daughter, and I hope that one day—'

'Don't speak to me of love, Mr Copperfield!' cried Mr Spenlow. 'You are both much too young! We'll throw these letters in the fire, and you must promise to forget the whole thing. There is no question of your marrying Dora!'

'But sir, I can't forget her! I love her!' I protested.

'That is my last word, Mr Copperfield! When you have time to consider, you'll realize it's wiser to do as I say. Now go to your work!'

I spent all day thinking of poor sweet Dora, and how she must be feeling. In the evening I hurried round to Miss Mills's house, but although she spoke wisely of love and broken hearts, she could not offer me any practical advice.

The next day, after a sleepless night, I arrived at the office at the normal time, and discovered all the clerks standing talking at the front door. This was so unusual that I stopped to ask what had happened.

'Why, don't you know?' asked one of them. 'The police have found Mr Spenlow dead!' I fell back, shocked.

'You look very pale, Mr Copperfield!' said another. 'Sit down here, sir!'

'Tell me – tell me what happened,' I gasped.

'Well, he went into town to dinner last night, and the carriage and horses came back at midnight without him. He was driving himself, you see. So the servants went to look for him, and found him dead in the road. He must have been ill, and have fallen out of the carriage. Anyway, he was dead when they found him.'

This was a terrible shock to me. Perhaps his anger with me had made him ill. In that case I was partly to blame for his death. But I am sorry to say I was also jealous of Dora's sadness. While she was crying for her dead father, she was not thinking of *me*, and I selfishly wanted to be the only person in her life.

In the next few weeks I became quite desperate because I could not see or speak to my sweet Dora. Miss Mills reported that Dora cried all day, and when my name was mentioned, only sobbed more loudly and said, 'Oh poor dear Father! How wicked of me to keep a secret from him! Oh! Oh!' So I did not feel encouraged to visit her. Soon after her father's funeral, Dora was taken to live with her two aunts at Putney, in south London, where she seemed to be further away from me than ever.

My aunt, meanwhile, began to be seriously worried about my health, as I was getting more and more depressed. So she suggested I should go to Dover for a few days, to make sure that her house was still in good condition, and then to Canterbury, to visit the Wickfields. I agreed willingly, as I was always happy to see Agnes. It was easy to take a few days' holiday from my work at the lawcourts and with Dr Strong.

I was glad to find that the person who was renting my aunt's house in Dover was looking after it well. I was then free to continue my journey to Canterbury, that beautiful ancient city, which seemed very little changed since my schooldays. The soft, clean air made me feel better than I had done for weeks.

When I arrived at the Wickfields' house, I found Mr Micawber in Uriah Heep's old office. We were pleased to see each other, but we both felt a little embarrassed. I realized that he did not want to talk about confidential matters concerning the firm of Heep and Wickfield, and he knew that I disliked his employer, Heep. So conversation was difficult, and in the end I was glad to leave him, and go upstairs to look for Agnes.

I found her in her sitting-room, and she looked up at me with such a warm welcome in her smile that I was very moved.

'Ah, Agnes!' I said. 'I've missed you so much recently! You helped me such a lot in the old days that I suppose I never learnt to think for myself. I always feel I need your help and advice. I get into such trouble, and I get so worried, and have so little confidence in myself, but when I'm with you, you give me purpose! You make me strong! What is your secret, my dear adopted sister?'

Agnes gave me her hand, which I kissed, and she went on, in her sisterly way, to listen sympathetically as I told her everything that had happened in the past few weeks. As usual, she knew the right thing to do. She advised me to write to Dora's aunts, to ask if I could visit Dora occasionally, and she encouraged me in my hopes of marriage. I felt again that peace which Agnes always brought to me.

We had not been sitting together long when Mrs Heep came in. She did not leave us for a moment all that evening, and I wondered whether Uriah had told her to watch over us. Whenever I looked at Agnes's lovely face, I saw Mrs Heep's evil black eyes staring at me.

The next day, Mrs Heep did not leave Agnes and me alone

even for a minute. The Heeps, mother and son, seemed to me like two ugly great black birds hanging over the house, and they made me so uncomfortable that I went out for a walk in the afternoon. I was walking along a path near the house, wondering if I should warn Agnes about Uriah's plan of marriage, when I heard footsteps behind me, and turned to see Uriah himself running after me.

'Wait for me, Mr Copperfield!' he cried.

'Actually,' I said, 'I came out to be alone.'

'Ah!' he said, with his oily smile, 'you don't like my mother being there all the time, do you?'

'No, I don't,' I replied, not caring if I sounded rude.

'But you see,' he continued, 'in my humble position, I have to be very careful. I'm not married to my Agnes yet, and you're a dangerous rival, Mr Copperfield.'

'What!' I cried in disgust. 'You allow Miss Wickfield no peace in her own home because of me? Don't you realize I think of her as my very dear sister, nothing more? Let me tell you I am engaged to another lady! There! Is that enough for you?'

'Oh Mr Copperfield!' cried Uriah, gratefully shaking my hand with his cold fishy one. 'I'll tell Mother to stop watching you at once! Why didn't you tell me that before? I know you've never liked and trusted me, as I've liked *you*!'

We returned to the house together in silence. That evening after dinner, when Agnes and Mrs Heep had left us, Uriah said to Mr Wickfield, 'Let's have some wine, partner, and drink to young Mr Copperfield's health. It isn't often we have the pleasure of his company, is it, partner?'

I knew Uriah was deliberately encouraging Mr Wickfield to drink too much, but I saw that although Agnes's father was aware of his weakness, he could no longer stop himself. As the evening passed, I was disgusted to see that Uriah became more and more cheerful as Mr Wickfield became more and more drunk. Finally Uriah stood up with a glass in his hand.

'Come, partner!' he said with his evil smile. 'Let's drink to the health of the most beautiful woman in the world!'

Poor, broken Mr Wickfield looked for a moment at the picture of his dead wife on the wall, so similar to Agnes.

'I may be humble,' continued Uriah, 'but I admire, no, I love your daughter Agnes!'

Suddenly a horrible cry came from Mr Wickfield. He had stood up, and was screaming with anger. He behaved so wildly and desperately that I thought he had gone mad. 'My child and you, Heep! No, never! You've taken everything from me, my business, my good name, my home, but you'll never take *her*!'

'Perhaps I've said too much too soon,' said Uriah, looking uncomfortable. 'But you'll be sorry, partner, if you say any more! You need me, remember? You've got nothing without me! Remember that before you accuse me of anything!'

Just then the door opened and Agnes entered silently.

'You're not well, Father, come with me,' she whispered gently, and helped the ashamed old man out. I thought she must have heard what had been said.

Later that night she came to say goodnight to me in the sitting-room, where I was alone, reading.

'Agnes, my dear sister,' I said to her, 'promise me that you will never agree to marry that evil creature, for any reason!'

Through her tears she smiled calmly at me. 'Don't worry, brother, I'm not afraid of him. My duty is to take care of Father, and I trust in God for the rest. Goodnight, David.'

David gets married

When I returned to London, I was delighted to discover that Dora's aunts had decided to allow me to visit her. So every Saturday and Sunday I walked to their house in Putney, and spent the afternoons there. Sometimes Dora sang or played the guitar, sometimes we walked by the river, and sometimes I brought Traddles or my aunt with me. What happy times they were!

Mr Spenlow had seemed a very rich man to me, but when he died the lawyers discovered that Dora would not inherit much from him after all, as there were many debts to pay. So I did not feel worried that anyone would suspect me of marrying Dora for her money. Mr Spenlow's firm lost a lot of business after his death, and I realized I would have to find another profession. I had always been good at writing, so I continued as secretary to Dr Strong, and also began reporting what was said in parliament, for the daily newspapers. I even wrote some stories, which were published in magazines, and was very pleased with the money I was earning.

The months passed, and I reached my twenty-first birthday. Traddles was still studying to be a lawyer, and still hoping to marry 'the dearest girl in the world'. I had moved out of my flat into a pleasant little house, and at last Dora's aunts had agreed to our marriage. I was looking forward to the happiest day of my life. The next few days went by very fast in a mist of excitement and happiness. My aunt and Mr Dick moved into an even smaller house near mine, and Peggotty travelled from Yarmouth to be present at my wedding.

I had always wanted Agnes to meet Dora, so I was glad when

they met, the day before the wedding. It was beautiful to see Dora's pretty face next to Agnes's calm one, and Dora whispering her secrets into Agnes's ears, as a child does to its mother. But after Agnes had gone to see my aunt, Dora said seriously to me, when we were alone, 'Perhaps if I'd had Agnes as a friend when I was younger, David dear, I wouldn't be so foolish and silly.'

'But I love you as you are, Dora!' I replied.

'I wonder why you ever fell in love with me!'

'Because nobody can see you, and not fall in love with you!'

'But if you'd never seen me, David, I wonder who you'd have married . . .'

I laughed and kissed her pretty lips, and she was soon as cheerful as usual again.

I cannot remember much about the wedding, except Dora by my side, in her beautiful dress and with a blushing face. Only when we were driving away from Putney together, did I wake from the dream. I believed it at last! It was my dear little wife I was sitting next to, whom I loved so much!

It seemed strange to return from our week's holiday and to find myself in my own small house with Dora. It was difficult to believe that we were going to spend the rest of our lives together. But soon I realized that married life was not as comfortable as it appeared. Neither Dora nor I knew anything about managing the house. We had a servant, of course, who managed *us*. She served our meals late, drank all our wine, and stole all our silver spoons. When she finally left, we had another who behaved in a similar way. I felt I had to speak to Dora about it.

'My love,' I began, 'couldn't you perhaps control the servants a little better?'

'David, don't be cross with your little Dora,' she said, coming to sit on my knee. But I wanted to show I could be firm.

'My sweet Dora, I really do think you should do something. I mean, yesterday I had no supper at all because the beef was burnt, and last week, when Traddles came to dinner, the meat wasn't cooked at all!'

'You knew before you married me what a silly girl I am! You shouldn't have married me if you were going to be angry with me! I don't think you love me at all!' And large tears ran down her pretty little face.

'Dora, my love! Of course I love you! Don't cry!' I could not continue our conversation then. But when she was calmer, and had dried her tears, she said very seriously, 'David, will you do something for me? Will you call me your child-wife?'

'Whatever do you mean, my dearest?' I asked in surprise.

'Just that, whenever you feel I'm being very foolish, you should remember that I'm like a child, not as clever as you, or anyone else. Don't be disappointed with me, just remember that your child-wife loves you very, very much.'

Of all the conversations we had, I remember that one very clearly. It made a strong impression on me, and I am glad now that I did not try to change Dora any more. I had fallen in love with an innocent child-like girl, and I could not expect her to become a wise, experienced woman in such a short time. But this meant that I had to carry all our problems on my own shoulders, and sometimes I felt sorry that I did not have a real partner in life, with whom to share these worries.

At about this time, my first book was published, and was a great success. Dora and my aunt were equally proud of me. I was becoming, however, rather worried about Dora. She had been ill for some time, and did not seem to be getting better. She was not strong, and could not walk anywhere by herself. I began to carry her downstairs every morning, and upstairs every night, and my aunt came every day to look after her. My little wife was still very pretty, and cheerful, but I knew how light she was, and how weak. I began to fear she would not be with me for much longer.

Early one morning when I was walking in the garden, I saw Daniel Peggotty opening the gate and coming towards me. His clothes were dusty, and he looked older than before, with white hair escaping untidily from under his hat. But his face was brown, and he looked healthy and strong.

'Master David!' he said gladly, when he saw me. 'I've come to tell you – you were always our friend – I've found her!'

'You've found little Emily!' I cried delightedly. 'But where – and how?'

'I heard she'd travelled with that wicked Steerforth to Italy, and lived there for a while. But in the end he became tired of her, and left her. She didn't know what to do, or where to go, poor thing! But she came back to London. And that's where I found my dear child! Because I've been all over Europe looking for her, but I knew she'd come back to England one day. So every night I've been searching the city streets for her. And last night I found her, hopeless and exhausted, on a bridge looking down into the river. If I hadn't found her then, I don't like to think what she would have done! But God was looking after my dear girl, and she's safe with me now.' He passed his strong hand over his eyes, and smiled at me. 'I've planned what we'll do, Master David, and I want to tell you about it. Emily and I are going to Australia. It's a new country, where nobody knows anything about her past. We'll be able to start a new life together. We'll be leaving in about six weeks.'

'Very sensible,' I said. 'And what about the rest of your family? Are Ham and Peggotty going to Australia too?'

'No, they aren't. Poor Ham will never be the same again. I really think his heart is broken. But he's got a good job, and is very popular in Yarmouth, so he'll stay there. My sister wants to stay too, partly because of you, Master David, and partly to look after Ham. She cooks and cleans for him in Yarmouth, you know.'

'Well, my friend,' I said, shaking hands firmly with the old boatman, 'I wish you and Emily all the best in your new life.'

'I'll do my duty, whether I'm in England or Australia,' said Daniel. 'And I'll never be separated from my little Emily again!'

⑩

Death and discovery

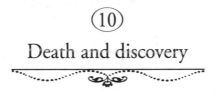

Traddles and I had both received rather strange letters from Mr Micawber, in which he asked us to come to Canterbury, with my aunt. At this meeting, he said, he would show to all of us the proof of Uriah Heep's wickedness. Dora was too ill to come with us, so Traddles, my aunt, Mr Dick and I travelled to Canterbury by coach, spent the night in a hotel there, and arrived punctually at the Wickfields' house the next morning. Mr Micawber met us at the door and showed us into Uriah Heep's office. Uriah himself seemed rather surprised to see us, but pretended to welcome us as old friends. Mr Micawber brought Agnes into the room too, and then stood firmly by the door.

'Don't wait, Micawber,' said Uriah to his assistant.

But Mr Micawber did not move. He stared coldly at his employer.

'Did you hear what I said, Micawber?' said Uriah angrily, his little eyes becoming redder while his long face went very pale.

'Yes!' replied Micawber. 'But I don't choose to leave. Listen to me, Heep! I don't care if I lose my job! I don't wish to work any longer for the wickedest man in England!'

Uriah fell back, shocked. Looking slowly round at us, with a dark, evil expression on his face, he said, 'I see! You've all arranged this between you! But I know who to blame for this! It's you, Copperfield! You're jealous of my new position, aren't you? But I know things about all of you which I can use against you – for example, I know about your father's business mistakes, Miss Agnes, and I know about your past in the warehouse, Copperfield! So be careful, I warn you all!'

'Mr Micawber,' I said calmly, 'please tell us what you were going to say about this man!'

Just then Traddles, who had disappeared a few minutes before, reappeared with Mrs Heep. Uriah had not noticed Traddles before. 'Who are you?' he demanded angrily.

'I am a lawyer and a friend of Mr Wickfield, sir,' said Traddles, in a businesslike way. 'And he's asked me to carry out all his business arrangements from now on.' This came as a surprise to me as well as to Uriah.

'The old fool has been drinking too much again!' said Uriah, looking uglier than ever. 'You can't believe anything he says! And you've bribed my assistant, I suppose, to speak against me!'

'It's you who have been dishonest,' said Traddles firmly, 'as we shall hear from Mr Micawber.' And we all looked expectantly towards that large, important-looking gentleman. He was clearly delighted to have such an interested audience, and cleared his throat several times before starting to speak. As he spoke, his voice became louder and louder with excitement, until he was almost shouting.

'Ladies and gentlemen,' he began, 'when very poor and desperate for work, I came to Canterbury as assistant to this evil man Heep. I am sorry to say I was soon involved in all his wicked plans. I may be poor, but I can't accept his lies, his cheating, his bribes and all the rest of it. And so I've brought you here today, ladies and gentlemen, to hear me accuse Heep publicly! One, he has confused and lied to his partner so often that poor Mr Wickfield now thinks he has himself been dishonest. Two, he has sometimes copied Mr Wickfield's signature on to false documents and cheques. Three, for years he has been stealing large amounts of money from Mr Wickfield and the firm!'

'You can never prove it!' cried Uriah wildly.

'I have taken copies of all the necessary documents,' said Mr Micawber confidently, 'while working as your clerk. And just to make sure, I've given them to Mr Traddles to keep safely.'

'Uriah, my dear boy,' cried his mother, sobbing bitterly, 'tell them how humble you are! Say you didn't mean to hurt anyone! Say you're sorry, and arrange matters with these gentlemen! Do, dear boy!'

'Mother, be quiet!' he whispered angrily. 'Don't help my enemies! Copperfield here would have given you a hundred pounds to say what you've just said!'

Suddenly my aunt attacked Uriah, hitting his head with her umbrella. 'Give me back my investments!' she cried. 'I thought Mr Wickfield had lost my money, and I didn't want to hurt Agnes by saying so! But now I know *you*'ve had control of the firm, and *you*'ve stolen my money . . .' Somehow I managed to get her away from him before she hurt him too badly.

Then Mrs Heep fell on her knees to all of us, begging us to forgive her dear boy, and to remember how humble he always was.

'Be silent, Mother!' said her son. He turned to Traddles and asked unpleasantly, 'Well? What are you asking me to do?'

'Not asking, *demanding*, Heep. You will give us the keys to all your boxes and drawers, all your documents and chequebooks, everything in fact that belongs to the firm. You will stay in this house until we've checked all the documents.'

'And if I don't agree?' he asked, frowning.

'Copperfield, perhaps you would fetch a couple of policemen. Things move slowly in the lawcourts, but in the end Mr Wickfield will get his business back, and you, Heep, will be in prison for a very long time.'

Uriah realized that he had to do what we wanted, and went to fetch the documents, with Mr Dick at his side. At the door, with his blackest, most evil expression, Heep turned and said to me, 'I've always hated you, Copperfield!' Then he was taken away.

In the next few days Traddles and Micawber worked very hard together to put right what Uriah had done. They discovered my aunt's money and gave it back to her, and paid all the firm's debts. Mr Wickfield decided to sell his business, and retire. The Wickfields would not have much money, but at least they did not owe anything. In the end Uriah Heep and his mother left Canterbury, but we all thought he was too evil to stay out of trouble for long.

My aunt had a wonderful idea for the Micawber family. 'Have you ever thought of going to live in Australia?' she suggested. 'It's a new country, with a lot of business opportunities.'

Mr Micawber was very interested. 'Something could easily turn up *there*,' he agreed. My aunt generously offered to lend him the necessary money to pay for the journey, and the whole Micawber family started planning and packing immediately.

When I returned to London, I realized my poor Dora was much worse. She stayed upstairs all the time now, and the sitting-room seemed very quiet without my little child-wife in her usual place. One day when I was sitting with her in her room, she said lovingly, 'You know, David dear, I'm afraid I was too young.'

'Don't say that, Dora!' I whispered, conscious that she was speaking of herself in the past.

'I was a silly little girl, David, and you know it. It's just as well that I won't live much longer. Perhaps if I lived, you'd wish you'd married someone more sensible, more practical, someone like ...' She did not finish what she was saying.

'But we've been so happy, Dora!' I said, trying not to cry.

She took my hand and kissed it. 'We have, haven't we? David, do you think if you asked Agnes, she'd come and see me? I have something particular to say to her.'

'Of course, my love, I'll write to her tonight.'

Agnes came the next day, and went straight upstairs to see Dora. Although the doctor and my aunt had told me there was no hope that Dora would live, when I held her hand and saw her love for me in her innocent blue eyes, I could not believe she would be taken from me. But when Agnes came downstairs so calmly and silently, and said nothing, but raised her hand and pointed upwards, I knew! It was over, and I remembered only darkness for a long time afterwards.

In the middle of my terrible sadness I received a message from Emily. She asked me to take a letter from her to Ham – her last words to the man who had loved her so much – before she and

Daniel left England for Australia. They were sailing in two weeks' time, and the Micawbers were going on the same ship. I remembered my childish love for little Emily, and agreed to do what she asked.

The weather was very stormy as I travelled through the night to Yarmouth. Several times the coach was almost knocked off the road by the wind and the rain. By the time we arrived in Yarmouth, most of the local people were in the streets, afraid to stay in their houses, in case the roof or the chimney blew down. Many women were crying, afraid for their husbands or brothers who were out fishing in their small boats. The sea itself, with its huge waves crashing noisily on the beach, frightened us all very much.

I went to the hotel, and tried to sleep a little after my tiring journey. But the wind made so much noise that I could not sleep, and I went down to the beach again, where a lot of people were standing together, watching the waves. By now the storm had got even worse.

'Two ships have gone down, sir!' a local fisherman shouted to me. 'A few miles away! We couldn't save any of the men on them! The waves were too high! And look! There's another!'

And suddenly I gasped in horror. I could see a great ship, which had been pushed violently on to the rocks by the waves. It was in danger of falling back into the waves, or of breaking in half, at any moment. Several figures were visible on the ship, especially one very active, curly-haired young man, who seemed to be giving orders. The crowd on the beach cried out as the ship rolled and a huge wave swept over it, carrying the men into the rushing water. In a moment the only figure we could see was the curly-haired young man, holding desperately on to the side of the ship and calling for help. What could we do? It was certain death for any man to enter those waves.

Just then I saw Ham Peggotty running through the crowd to the edge of the water. One end of a rope was tied around his waist, and the other end was held firmly by three strong men standing on the beach.

'No, Ham!' I cried, trying to hold him back. 'Don't try to rescue that poor sailor! You'll kill yourself!'

'Let me go, Master David!' he replied cheerfully, shaking both my hands. 'If God thinks it's time for me to die, then I'm ready! Friends, I'm going in! Give me more rope!'

He dived in under a great wave, and swam strongly towards the ship. In another moment he would have reached it, when a high green hill of water appeared, and the ship went down with a great crash. The people on the beach pulled on Ham's rope, and he arrived at my feet – dead. They carried him to the nearest house, and I called a doctor, but nothing could be done for him. He had been beaten to death by that great wave, and his generous heart had stopped for ever.

As I sat hopelessly by his bed, a fisherman who had known me when Emily and I were children, came to tell me he recognized the curly-haired sailor, whose body had been thrown out of the water by the waves. I went to see. And there on the beach where she and I had played, I saw Steerforth lying, with his handsome face on his arm. He would never smile at me or Emily again.

I was surrounded by too many ghosts to return to London and my old life. I was selfishly sad that I had lost my child-wife and my childhood friend, and sometimes I felt I wanted to die. So I left England, and travelled for many months in Europe. I lived in a dark, miserable dream, with no hope or interest in my future.

He dived in under a great wave.

One evening I arrived in a village in Switzerland, and received a packet of letters that had been waiting for me. The first one I opened was from Agnes. She gave me no advice, but she told me simply that she trusted me to find a purpose in life, and that she would always be proud of me, and love me as a sister.

As the light died out of the sky, and I watched the colour of the snow on the mountain tops change, I felt I was waking from my unhappy dream, and I began to understand how much I loved Agnes. She had been the one who had always guided and supported me, and now I realized I needed her love for the rest of my life. Had falling in love with Dora been a mistake? We had both been very young, it is true. I had always called Agnes sister, and now perhaps I no longer had the right to ask whether her love for me was more than sisterly.

However, I decided to return, and travelled home to England, after three years of absence. I was delighted to find that Traddles had married his Sophy, and was doing well as a lawyer. My aunt had moved back to her old Dover house, and was living happily there with Mr Dick and Peggotty. When I visited my aunt, I took the opportunity of asking her about Agnes.

'Has she – has she any young man she'd like to marry?' I asked as lightly as possible.

My aunt looked carefully at me as she replied, 'I suspect she has, David. She's never mentioned it to me, but I think – I feel sure she's going to marry soon.'

I was firm with myself and did not show my feelings. I borrowed a horse and rode to Canterbury to ask Agnes myself. When I saw that beautiful, gentle face again, I knew I had come home. I knew how dear she was to me, and would always be.

'Agnes,' I said, 'I am so grateful to you, for making me what

I am, for helping me to be good! But I think you have a secret. Let me share it, Agnes, as your brother! Tell me whom you love!'

Agnes turned away from me and burst into tears. Somehow these tears did not sadden me, but gave me hope. 'My dear Agnes! Don't cry!'

'David, leave me! I can't talk about it now!' she sobbed.

'Agnes, you're dearer to me than anything in the world. Don't think I'll be jealous of any man you choose to marry. I only want you to be happy!'

She had stopped crying now and was calmer. 'If I have a secret, David, it is – not a new one. It has been my secret – for a long time!'

I was wild with hope. 'Not a new one'! Did she mean ...? 'Dearest Agnes! Dare I hope to call you more than a sister!' She was in my arms and sobbing again, but this time with happiness. 'I went away, Agnes, loving you! I returned home, loving you!'

We held each other for some time, sure now of each other's love.

'There is something I must tell you, David,' she said gently, looking calmly into my face. 'I have loved you all my life!' She added, 'And something else – before our sweet Dora died, she asked me – can you guess – to fill the empty place in your heart.' And Agnes laid her head on my shoulder, and cried. And I cried with her, although we were both so happy.

My story has almost come to an end. I have published several books now, and am a well-known writer. Agnes and I have been married for twenty years, and live in perfect happiness, with our children around us. We have heard from Daniel Peggotty in Australia. He and Emily have made friends there and are happy.

Mr Micawber has become an important figure in a large Australian town, and his family are quite used to living there. My aunt, Mr Dick and Peggotty are all white-haired and old now, but still very fit, and they love playing with our children whenever they can. My old friend Traddles has two sons of his own, and will soon become a judge.

When I think of my friends and family, Agnes's lovely face shines above them all. She is here, next to me, as I write, and I hope that when my life comes to its end, she will be with me in the shadows, pointing upwards to the light!

Exercises

A Checking your understanding

Chapters 1–2 *How much can you remember? Check your answers.*
1 What was Mrs Copperfield's, and her servant's, first name?
2 Which town did Daniel Peggotty live in?
3 How long was David kept locked in his room after his beating?
4 How much money did Peggotty give David?
5 What was Barkis's message to Peggotty?
6 Who collected David from the coach station in London?
7 What was the name of David's school?
8 What was the headmaster's name?
9 Who was the unluckiest boy in the school?
10 What was different about David's home when he returned?

Chapters 3–5 *Are these sentences true (T) or false (F)?*
1 After Mrs Copperfield's death Peggotty was asked to stay
   on as the Murdstones' servant.
2 David started work in the warehouse at the age of twelve.
3 Mrs Micawber was not used to having so little money.
4 Miss Betsey Trotwood recognized David as soon as she saw him.
5 Mr Dick's suggestions were all very practical.
6 Dr Strong's boarding school was in Dover.
7 Steerforth was studying at Oxford University.
8 Mr Wickfield asked Uriah Heep to become his partner.

B Working with language

1 *Put this summary of Chapter 6 in the right order, and then join the*
   parts together to make five sentences.
   1 that he wanted to marry Agnes one day
   2 the day after Barkis's funeral Ham brought the terrible news
   3 David returned to Yarmouth
   4 he explained to David
   5 soon afterwards David met Tommy Traddles and the Micawbers

6 when Uriah Heep came to David's rooms for coffee
7 in order to help his old friend Peggotty
8 that Emily had run away with Steerforth
9 and immediately fell in love with Dora Spenlow
10 whose husband, Barkis, was dying
11 one day David was invited to Mr Spenlow's house
12 who were delighted to see him again

2 *Put together these beginnings and endings of sentences.*
Check your answers in Chapter 7.
1 Sitting next to Dora was a young lady
2 I was very surprised
3 I did not notice the dust,
4 Miss Mills said nothing,
5 I told her
6 If I had only known then,
7 but smiled kindly on us both.
8 I would die without her.
9 to see my aunt coming upstairs.
10 what I discovered long afterwards!
11 or the road we were taking.
12 I had not noticed before.

C Activities

1 Write Julia Mills's diary for the day when David explained to Dora that he no longer had any money (Chapter 8).
2 Do you think David was right to marry Dora? Why did he not think of marrying Agnes until later?
What would you have done in his situation? Write an essay giving your opinions.
3 You are a Yarmouth newspaper reporter. Write a report of the storm, the shipwreck and Ham's rescue attempt (Chapter 10).

Glossary

admire to look at with pleasure, to like

adopt to take another person's child into your own family to become your own child, or to feel that someone is part of your family

amount quantity or sum (of money)

angel a spirit or messenger from God, or a kind, pure, beautiful woman

approve to think or say that something or someone is good or right

blush (*v*) to become red in the face, especially when embarrassed

boarding school a school where pupils board, i.e. eat and sleep as well as study

carriage a smart coach pulled by horses

cart an open wagon pulled by one or more horses

churchyard ground near a church where dead people are buried

coach a carriage pulled by horses, especially for long journeys and public transport

creditor someone to whom money is owed

curly-haired of someone whose hair grows in curls or round shapes

debt money that should be paid to someone

disgust (*n*) a strong feeling of dislike

document written or printed paper with important information

drunk (*adj*) of someone who has drunk too much alcohol

embarrassed worried about what other people think, ashamed of something

evil (*adj*) not good, wicked; (*n*) great wickedness

excuse (*n*) an explanation for doing something

firm (*adj*) strong and determined in behaviour

firm (*n*) a company or business

funeral the ceremony in which a dead person is buried

future (*n*) the time that is coming

gentleman a man of good family, usually wealthy

Good heavens! an exclamation of surprise

headmaster the man in charge of a school

humble not proud of yourself

invest to put money into a bank or business

lawcourts the place where judges and lawyers listen to law cases
marriage the time when a man and a woman are married
Master used when speaking to a boy or young gentleman
opportunity a chance, the right moment
orphan a child whose parents are dead
pale with a white face
parliament the place where a country's laws are discussed and made
partner a person who works with another in a shared business
picnic (*n*) a meal which is eaten in the open air somewhere away
  from home
plain (*adj*) not pretty, ordinary-looking
publish to prepare a book for selling
retire to stop work when you become old
right (*n*) being able or allowed to do something
rival someone who tries to take what you want
ruin (*n*) (here) the loss of her good name
servant someone who is paid to do housework
shilling a British coin no longer in use (there were twenty shillings
  in a pound)
sob (*v*) to cry loudly and very unhappily
stepfather a man who marries your mother after your father's death
stern (*adj*) unsmiling, a little angry
trust (*v*) to have confidence in someone
turn up to come or arrive
twins two children who are born to the same mother at the same time
warehouse a building where you store goods
wicked of bad character
wise knowing what is right and good